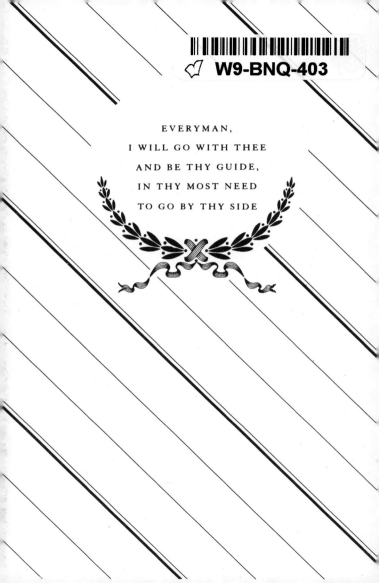

W9-BNQ-403

EVERYMAN,
I WILL GO WITH THEE
AND BE THY GUIDE,
IN THY MOST NEED
TO GO BY THY SIDE

EVERYMAN'S LIBRARY
POCKET POETS

FATHERHOOD

POEMS ABOUT FATHERS

••••••••••••••••••••

SELECTED AND EDITED BY
CARMELA CIURARU

EVERYMAN'S LIBRARY
POCKET POETS

Alfred A. Knopf New York London Toronto

THIS IS A BORZOI BOOK
PUBLISHED BY ALFRED A. KNOPF

This selection by Carmela Ciuraru first published in
Everyman's Library, 2007
Copyright © 2007 by Everyman's Library

A list of acknowledgments to copyright owners appears at the back
of this volume.

US website: www.randomhouse.com/everymans

ISBN 978-0-307-26458-9 (US)
1-84159-771-6 & 978-84159-771-3 (UK)

A CIP catalogue record for this book is available from the British Library

Typography by Peter B. Willberg
Typeset in the UK by AccComputing, North Barrow, Somerset
Printed and bound in Germany by GGP Media GmbH, Pössneck

Pm 13.00 9/07

CONTENTS

Foreword 13

BECOMING: ON BIRTH AND INFANCY

THOMAS DEKKER
    "Golden slumbers kiss your eyes" 19

ALGERNON CHARLES SWINBURNE Étude Réaliste   20

ALFRED, LORD TENNYSON
    "Sweet and low, sweet and low" 22

W. B. YEATS A Cradle Song 23

WILLIAM BLAKE Infant Joy 24

WILLIAM BLAKE Infant Sorrow 25

SU TUNG-P'O On the Birth of His Son 26

GEORGE MACDONALD The Baby 27

SIDNEY LANIER Baby Charley 29

D. H. LAWRENCE A Baby Asleep After Pain . . 30

WILLIAM BLAKE A Cradle Song 31

SAMUEL TAYLOR COLERIDGE
    Sonnet: On Receiving a Letter Informing
    Me of the Birth of a Son 33

SAMUEL TAYLOR COLERIDGE
    From Frost at Midnight 34

SAMUEL TAYLOR COLERIDGE To an Infant 36

RUDYARD KIPLING Seal Lullaby 37

WILLIAM CANTON Laus Infantium 38

KENNETH REXROTH The American Century . . 39

RICHARD MURPHY Natural Son 40

SIR WALTER SCOTT Lullaby of an Infant Chief 41

GALWAY KINNELL The Olive Wood Fire 42

DONALD HALL My Son My Executioner 43

DAUGHTER TO FATHER

GJERTRUD SCHNACKENBERG Supernatural Love 47

ANNE BRADSTREET

    To Her Father with Some Verses 50

HENRY CLAY WORK Come Home, Father! 51

NAOMI SHIHAB NYE

    My Father and the Figtree 53

SOPHIE CABOT BLACK To Her Father 55

DEBORA GREGER The Armorer's Daughter . . 57

GWEN HARWOOD For My Father 59

LOUISE GLÜCK Snow 60

SOPHIE CABOT BLACK Turning Away 61

KATHA POLLITT A Chinese Bowl 62

ELIZABETH BARRETT BROWNING

    To My Father on His Birthday 65

HARRYETTE MULLEN Father (Part 1) 66

DEBORAH GARRISON

    Dad, You Returned to Me This Morning 67

NATASHA TRETHEWEY Amateur Fighter 69

SOPHIE CABOT BLACK Brunnhilde, to Her Father 71

FATHERS AND SONS

HOMER *From* The Iliad, Book VI 75

WILLIAM SHAKESPEARE *From* Henry IV, Part 2 76

THOMAS BAILEY ALDRICH Alec Yeaton's Son . . 77

FRANK L. STANTON Mighty Like a Rose 80

THOMAS BASTARD De Puero Balbutiente 81

PERCY BYSSHE SHELLEY To William Shelley . . 82

ALGERNON CHARLES SWINBURNE
    "Child, when they say that others" 85

WILLIAM WORDSWORTH Anecdote for Fathers 87

COVENTRY PATMORE The Toys 90

THOMAS HOOD A Parental Ode to My Son, Aged
    Three Years and Five Months 92

GERARD MANLEY HOPKINS
    The Child Is Father to the Man 95

TED HUGHES Dust as We Are 96

SEAMUS HEANEY Follower 98

SEAMUS HEANEY Digging 100

SEAMUS HEANEY The Nod 102

GALWAY KINNELL
    After Making Love We Hear Footsteps . . 103

HOWARD NEMEROV
    September, the First Day of School 105

JOHN BERRYMAN *From* Dream Songs 107

WILLIAM STAFFORD Listening 108

EUGENE FIELD
    Inscription for My Little Son's Silver Plate 109

ANDREW HUDGINS
 Elegy for My Father, Who Is Not Dead .. 110
MICHAEL LONGLEY The Branch 111
CZESLAW MILOSZ Father in the Library 112
CZESLAW MILOSZ Father's Incantations 113
YEHUDA AMICHAI
 My Son, My Son, My Head, My Head 114
JOSEPH BRODSKY Odysseus to Telemachus 115
LOUISE GLÜCK Telemachus' Fantasy   117
BORIS PASTERNAK Hamlet 119
RUSSELL EDSON The Changeling   120
RAYMOND CARVER Photograph of My Father in
 His Twenty-second Year 122
JASON SHINDER The Past   123
MURRAY JACKSON Gifts 124
RICHARD WILBUR
 My Father Paints the Summer 126

FATHER TO DAUGHTER

WILLIAM SHAKESPEARE From King Lear   131
CHARLES KINGSLEY To a Child 132
BEN JONSON On My First Daughter 133
ROBERT BURNS A Poet's Welcome to His Love-
 begotten Daughter 134
PERCY BYSSHE SHELLEY To Ianthe 136
MARK STRAND For Jessica, My Daughter 137
STEPHEN SPENDER To My Daughter   139

GEORGE OPPEN Sara in Her Father's Arms 140
TED HUGHES Full Moon and Little Frieda 141
RICHARD WILBUR The Writer 142
W. B. YEATS A Prayer for My Daughter 144

GRANDFATHERS
ELIZABETH BISHOP For Grandfather 151
W. S. MERWIN
    Grandfather in the Old Men's Home 152
SARA TEASDALE Grandfather's Love 153
ANDREW WATERHOUSE
    Climbing My Grandfather 154
ROBERT LOWELL Dunbarton 155
MEGHAN O'ROURKE
    Elegy for a Grandfather 158
CHARLES REZNIKOFF My Grandfather, Dead
    Long Before I Was Born 159
DONALD HALL Maple Syrup 160

SORROW, FURY, REGRET
WILLIAM BLAKE The Little Boy Lost 165
THOMAS CAMPBELL Lord Ullin's Daughter 166
STANLEY KUNITZ The Portrait 169
HENRI COLE Radiant Ivory 170
C. D. WRIGHT Tours 171
THEODORE ROETHKE My Papa's Waltz 172
EDWARD LUCIE-SMITH The Lesson 173

LUCILLE CLIFTON cigarettes 174

MEGHAN O'ROURKE Ohio 175

JAMES TATE The Lost Pilot 176

LOUIS SIMPSON

 My Father in the Night Commanding No 179

SYLVIA PLATH Daddy 181

WILLIAM JAY SMITH American Primitive 185

HOWARD MOSS Elegy for My Father 186

ELEGIES: ILLNESS, LOSS, AND LETTING GO

BEN JONSON On My First Son 191

JOHN BEAUMONT

 To My Dear Son, Gervase Beaumont 192

THOMAS GRAY Epitaph on a Child 193

ROBERT BURNS On My Ever Honoured Father 194

LOUISE GLÜCK Metamorphosis 195

SHARON OLDS Nullipara 198

SHARON OLDS His Terror 199

SHARON OLDS His Stillness 200

ROBERT HERRICK

 Epitaph upon a Child that Died 201

WILLIAM WORDSWORTH The Childless Father .. 202

ROBERT LOUIS STEVENSON

 God Gave to Me a Child in Part 203

JOHANN WOLFGANG VON GOETHE The Erl-King 204

GALWAY KINNELL Parkinson's Disease 206

PASCALE PETIT The Strait-jackets 208

TONY HOAGLAND Benevolence 209

SUSAN WICKS My Father Is Shrinking 211

MARY OLIVER Poem for My Father's Ghost .. 213

ELISE PASCHEN Threshold 215

ROBERT LOWELL
     Terminal Days at Beverly Farms 216

EAMON GRENNAN Walk, Night Falling, Memory
     of My Father 218

DONALD HALL White Apples 221

BRENDAN KENNELLY I See You Dancing, Father 222

DYLAN THOMAS
     Do Not Go Gentle into That Good Night 223

FRANCES ELLEN WATKINS The Drunkard's Child 224

W. S. MERWIN Strawberries 226

JOHN BERRYMAN *From* Dream Songs 227

MILLER WILLIAMS Vision in Black and White 228

SEAMUS HEANEY Seeing the Sick 229

MARK STRAND Elegy for My Father 230

Index of Authors 241

Acknowledgments 249

11

FOREWORD

Unlike the subject of motherhood, which has inspired some of the most sentimental poems ever written, fatherhood as literary fodder seems always to have provoked more ambivalence. (You can trace bereft sons all the way back to Homer.) According to a despairing John Berryman, in a poem from *Dream Songs* (#241), "father" is "the loneliest word in the one language."

In this anthology, memories of poignant moments abound, such as Yeats's "Cradle Song," whose last lines are adapted from a Gaelic song: "I kiss you and kiss you, / With arms round my own, / Ah, how shall I miss you, / When, dear, you have grown." "Man's breathing Miniature!" writes Coleridge, awestruck and humbled by his newborn child in the tender "To an Infant." The birth of a child yields moments of humor, too, as in the Chinese poet Su Tung-P'o's witty "On the Birth of His Son": "I, through intelligence, / Having wrecked my whole life, / Only hope the baby will prove / Ignorant and stupid. / Then he will crown a tranquil life / By becoming a Cabinet Minister."

A number of poems in this collection, especially those describing fathers and sons, convey a vulnerability rarely written about. In "Dust as We Are," Ted Hughes remembers caring for his ailing father, and Howard Nemerov offers a father's bittersweet perspective on dropping off his son at his classroom in "September, the First Day of School."

The bond between fathers and daughters can be especially strong. In Louise Glück's "Snow," the speaker recalls her father carrying her on his shoulders to see the circus: "My father liked / to stand like this, to hold me / so he couldn't see me." Katha Pollitt's "A Chinese Bowl" offers a quotidian scene of family life: a girl sits curled up on the floor writing a play called "Bean Soup and Rice," as her father sits at his desk immersed in his work: "I think, This is happiness," she writes.

Grandfathers make appearances as well, whether as a surrogate father (Robert Lowell's "Dunbarton") or as an influence from beyond the grave, as in Charles Reznikoff's brief poem "My Grandfather, Dead Long Before I was Born." Elizabeth Bishop's intimate, child-like "For Grandfather" is a wistful missive: "How far north are you by now?" she asks. "Where is your seal-skin cap with ear-lugs? / That old fur coat with the black frogs? / You'll catch your death again."

The section entitled "Sorrow, Fury, Regret" captures most pointedly the dramatic variability of the father–child relationship. Perhaps no poem is as explicit and powerful as Sylvia Plath's "Daddy," which describes an idealized yet oppressive father, one whom the speaker rejects with a resounding, forceful brutality. It is Plath's defining poetic utterance, and surely among the most searing poems ever written.

The book's final section explores loss – in some cases that of a father, and in others, perhaps the most painful loss of all, that of a child. In "On My First Son," Ben Jonson mourns his seven-year-old: "Farewell, thou child of my right hand, and joy; / My sin was too much hope of thee, loved boy.... Oh, could I lose all father, now!"

Writing as daughters and sons, and as fathers themselves, these poets convey the profound (and profoundly complicated) nature of the father–child bond. In some instances it is more fraught than loving; yet, as the poems here amply demonstrate, it can also provide lessons in forgiveness, reconciliation, gratitude, and love.

Carmela Ciuraru

BECOMING: ON
BIRTH AND INFANCY

"GOLDEN SLUMBERS
KISS YOUR EYES"

Golden slumbers kiss your eyes,
Smiles awake you when you rise.
Sleep, pretty wantons, do not cry,
And I will sing a lullaby:
Rock them, rock them, lullaby.

Care is heavy, therefore sleep you;
You are care, and care must keep you.
Sleep, pretty wantons, do not cry,
And I will sing a lullaby:
Rock them, rock them, lullaby.

THOMAS DEKKER (ATTRIB.)   19

ÉTUDE RÉALISTE

I

A baby's feet, like sea-shells pink,
   Might tempt, should Heaven see meet,
An angel's lips to kiss, we think,
    A baby's feet.

Like rose-hued sea-flowers toward the heat
   They stretch and spread and wink
Their ten soft buds that part and meet.

No flower-bells that expand and shrink
   Gleam half so heavenly sweet
As shine on life's untrodden brink
    A baby's feet.

II

A baby's hands, like rosebuds furled,
   Whence yet no leaf expands,
Ope if you touch, though close upcurled,
    A baby's hands.

Then, even as warriors grip their brands
   When battle's bolt is hurled,
They close, clenched hard like tightening bands.

No rosebuds yet by dawn impearled
    Match, even in loveliest lands,
The sweetest flowers in all the world –
    A baby's hands.

III

A baby's eyes, ere speech begin,
    Ere lips learn words or sighs,
Bless all things bright enough to win
    A baby's eyes.

Love, while the sweet thing laughs and lies,
    And sleep flows out and in,
Lies perfect in them Paradise.

Their glance might cast out pain and sin,
    Their speech make dumb the wise.
By mute glad godhead felt within
    A baby's eyes.

"SWEET AND LOW, SWEET AND LOW"

Sweet and low, sweet and low,
Wind of the western sea,
Low, low, breathe and blow,
Wind of the western sea!
Over the rolling waters go,
Come from the dying moon, and blow,
Blow him again to me;
While my little one, while my pretty one, sleeps.

Sleep and rest, sleep and rest,
Father will come to thee soon;
Rest, rest, on mother's breast,
Father will come to thee soon;
Father will come to his babe in the best,
Silver sails all out of the west,
Under the silver moon:
Sleep, my little one, sleep, my pretty one, sleep.

A CRADLE SONG

"Coth yani me von gilli beg,
'N heur ve thu more a creena."

The angels are bending
    Above your white bed,
They weary of tending
    The souls of the dead.

God smiles in high heaven
    To see you so good,
The old planets seven
    Grow gay with his mood.

I kiss you and kiss you,
    With arms round my own,
Ah, how shall I miss you,
    When, dear, you have grown.

INFANT JOY
From *Songs of Innocence*

"I have no name:
I am but two days old."
What shall I call thee?
"I happy am,
Joy is my name."
Sweet joy befall thee!

Pretty joy!
Sweet joy, but two days old.
Sweet Joy I call thee:
Thou dost smile,
I sing the while,
Sweet joy befall thee!

INFANT SORROW

My mother groaned, my father wept,
Into the dangerous world I leapt;
Helpless, naked, piping loud,
Like a fiend hid in a cloud.

Struggling in my father's hands,
Striving against my swaddling bands,
Bound and weary, I thought best
To sulk upon my mother's breast.

ON THE BIRTH OF HIS SON

Families, when a child is born
Want it to be intelligent.
I, through intelligence,
Having wrecked my whole life,
Only hope the baby will prove
Ignorant and stupid.
Then he will crown a tranquil life
By becoming a Cabinet Minister.

TRANSLATED BY ARTHUR WALEY

THE BABY

Where did you come from, baby dear?
Out of the everywhere into the here.

Where did you get your eyes so blue?
Out of the sky as I came through.

What makes the light in them sparkle and spin?
Some of the starry spikes left in.

Where did you get that little tear?
I found it waiting when I got here.

What makes your forehead so smooth and high?
A soft hand stroked it as I went by.

What makes your cheek like a warm white rose?
Something better than any one knows.

Whence that three-cornered smile of bliss?
Three angels gave me at once a kiss.

Where did you get that pearly ear?
God spoke, and it came out to hear.

Where did you get those arms and hands?
Love made itself into hooks and bands.

Feet, whence did you come, you darling things?
From the same box as the cherubs' wings.

How did they all just come to be you?
God thought about me, and so I grew.

But how did you come to us, you dear?
God thought of you, and so I am here.

BABY CHARLEY

He's fast asleep. See how, O Wife,
Night's finger on the lip of life
Bids whist the tongue, so prattle-rife,
Of busy Baby Charley.

One arm stretched backward round his head,
Five little toes from out the bed
Just showing, like five rosebuds red,
– So slumbers Baby Charley.

Heaven-lights, I know, are beaming through
Those lucent eyelids, veined with blue,
That shut away from mortal view
Large eyes of Baby Charley.

O sweet Sleep-Angel, throned now
On the round glory of his brow,
Wave thy wing and waft my vow
Breathed over Baby Charley.

I vow that my heart, when death is nigh,
Shall never shiver with a sigh
For act of hand or tongue or eye
That wronged my Baby Charley!

SIDNEY LANIER   29

A BABY ASLEEP AFTER PAIN

As a drenched, drowned bee
Hangs numb and heavy from a bending flower,
So clings to me
My baby, her brown hair brushed with wet tears
And laid against her cheek;
Her soft white legs hanging heavily over my arm
Swinging heavily to my movements as I walk.
My sleeping baby hangs upon my life,
Like a burden she hangs on me.
She has always seemed so light,
But now she is wet with tears and numb with pain
Even her floating hair sinks heavily,
Reaching downwards;
As the wings of a drenched, drowned bee
Are a heaviness, and a weariness.

A CRADLE SONG
From *Songs of Innocence*

Sweet dreams, form a shade
O'er my lovely infant's head;
Sweet dreams of pleasant streams
By happy, silent, moony beams.

Sweet Sleep, with soft down
Weave thy brows an infant crown.
Sweet Sleep, angel mild,
Hover o'er my happy child.

Sweet smiles, in the night
Hover over my delight;
Sweet smiles, mother's smiles,
All the livelong night beguiles.

Sweet moans, dovelike sighs,
Chase not slumber from thy eyes.
Sweet moans, sweeter smiles,
All the dovelike moans beguiles.

Sleep, sleep, happy child,
All creation slept and smil'd;
Sleep, sleep, happy sleep,
While o'er thee thy mother weep.

Sweet babe, in thy face
Holy image I can trace.
Sweet babe, once like thee,
Thy Maker lay, and wept for me,

Wept for me, for thee, for all,
When He was an infant small.
Thou His image ever see,
Heavenly face that smiles on thee,

Smiles on thee, on me, on all;
Who became an infant small.
Infant smiles are His own smiles;
Heaven and earth to peace beguiles.

SONNET: ON RECEIVING A LETTER INFORMING ME OF THE BIRTH OF A SON

When they did greet me Father, sudden Awe
Weigh'd down my spirit! I retired and knelt
Seeking the throne of grace, but inly felt
No heavenly visitation upwards draw
My feeble mind, nor cheering ray impart.
Ah me! before the Eternal Sire I brought
The unquiet silence of confused Thought
And shapeless feelings: my o'erwhelmed Heart
Trembled: & vacant tears stream'd down my face.
And now once more, O Lord! to thee I bend,
Lover of souls! and groan for future grace,
That, ere my Babe youth's perilous maze have trod,
Thy overshadowing Spirit may descend
And he be born again, a child of God!

From FROST AT MIDNIGHT

The Frost performs its secret ministry,
Unhelped by any wind. The owlet's cry
Came loud – and hark, again! loud as before.
The inmates of my cottage, all at rest,
Have left me to that solitude, which suits
Abstruser musings: save that at my side
My cradled infant slumbers peacefully.
'Tis calm indeed! so calm, that it disturbs
And vexes meditation with its strange
And extreme silentness. Sea, hill, and wood,
This populous village! Sea, and hill, and wood,
With all the numberless goings-on of life,
Inaudible as dreams! the thin blue flame
Lies on my low-burnt fire, and quivers not;
Only that film, which fluttered on the grate,
Still flutters there, the sole unquiet thing.
Methinks, its motion in this hush of nature
Gives it dim sympathies with me who live,
Making it a companionable form,
Whose puny flaps and freaks the idling Spirit
By its own moods interprets, every where
Echo or mirror seeking of itself,
And makes a toy of Thought.

. . .

Dear Babe, that sleepest cradled by my side,
Whose gentle breathings, heard in this deep calm,
Fill up the interspersed vacancies
And momentary pauses of the thought!
My babe so beautiful! it thrills my heart
With tender gladness, thus to look at thee,
And think that thou shalt learn far other lore,
And in far other scenes! For I was reared
In the great city, pent 'mid cloisters dim,
And saw nought lovely but the sky and stars.
But *thou*, my babe! shalt wander like a breeze
By lakes and sandy shores...

Therefore all seasons shall be sweet to thee,
Whether the summer clothe the general earth
With greenness, or the redbreast sit and sing
Betwixt the tufts of snow on the bare branch
Of mossy apple-tree, while the night thatch
Smokes in the sun-thaw; whether the eave-drops fall
Heard only in the trances of the blast,
Or if the secret ministry of frost
Shall hang them up in silent icicles,
Quietly shining to the quiet Moon.

SAMUEL TAYLOR COLERIDGE   35

TO AN INFANT

Ah cease thy Tears and Sobs, my little Life!
I did but snatch away the unclasp'd Knife:
Some safer Toy will soon arrest thine eye,
And to quick Laughter change this peevish cry!
Poor Stumbler on the rocky coast of Woe,
Tutor'd by Pain each source of Pain to know!
Alike the foodful fruit and scorching fire
Awake thy eager grasp and young desire:
Alike the Good, the Ill offend thy sight,
And rouse the stormy Sense of shrill Affright!
Untaught, yet wise! mid all thy brief alarms
Thou closely clingest to thy Mother's arms,
Nestling thy little face in that fond breast
Whose anxious Heavings lull thee to thy rest!
Man's breathing Miniature! thou mak'st me sigh –
A Babe art thou – and such a Thing am I!
To anger rapid and as soon appeas'd,
For trifles mourning and by trifles pleas'd,
Break Friendship's Mirror with a tetchy blow,
Yet snatch what coals of fire on Pleasure's altar glow!
O thou that rearest with celestial aim
The future Seraph in my mortal frame,
Thrice holy FAITH! whatever thorns I meet
As on I totter with unpractis'd feet,
Still let me stretch my arms and cling to thee,
Meek Nurse of Souls through their long infancy!

SEAL LULLABY

Oh! hush thee, my baby, the night is behind us,
    And black are the waters that sparkled so green.
The moon, o'er the combers, looks downward to find us
    At rest in the hollows that rustle between.
Where billow meets billow, there soft by the pillow;
    Ah, weary wee flipperling, curl at thy ease!
The storm shall not wake thee, nor shark overtake thee,
    Asleep in the arms of the slow-swinging seas.

LAUS INFANTIUM

In praise of little children I will say
God first made man, then found a better way
For woman, but his third way was the best.
Of all created things, the loveliest
And most divine are children. Nothing here
Can be to us more gracious or more dear.
And though, when God saw all his works were good,
There was no rosy flower of babyhood,
'Twas said of children in a later day
That none could enter Heaven save such as they.

The earth, which feels the flowering of a thorn,
Was glad, O little child, when you were born;
The earth, which thrills when skylarks scale the blue,
Soared up itself to God's own Heaven in you;

And Heaven, which loves to lean down and to glass
Its beauty in each dewdrop on the grass –
Heaven laughed to find your face so pure and fair,
And left, O little child, its reflex there.

THE AMERICAN CENTURY

Blackbirds whistle over the young
Willow leaves, pale celadon green,
In the cleft of the emerald hills.
My daughter is twenty-one months old.
Already she knows the names of
Many birds and flowers and all
The animals of barnyard and zoo.
She paddles in the stream, chasing
Tiny bright green frogs. She wants
To catch them and kiss them. Now she
Runs to me with a tuft of rose
Gray owl's clover. "What's that? Oh! What's that?"
She hoots like an owl and caresses
The flower when I tell her its name.
Overhead in the deep sky
Of May Day jet bombers cut long
White slashes of smoke. The blackbird
Sings and the baby laughs, midway
In the century of horror.

NATURAL SON

Before the spectacled professor snipped
The cord, I heard your birth-cry flood the ward,
And lowered your mother's tortured head, and wept.
The house you'd left would need to be restored.

No worse pain could be borne, to bear the joy
Of seeing you come in a slow dive from the womb,
Pushed from your fluid home, pronounced "a boy".
You'll never find so well equipped a room.

No house we build could hope to satisfy
Every small need, now that you've made this move
To share our loneliness, much as we try
Our vocal skill to wall you round with love.

This day you crave so little, we so much
For you to live, who need our merest touch.

LULLABY OF AN INFANT CHIEF

O hush thee, my babie, thy sire was a knight,
Thy mother a lady, both lovely and bright;
The woods and the glens, from the towers which we see,
They all are belonging, dear babie, to thee.
O ho ro, i ri ri, cadul gu lo,
O ho ro, i ri ri, cadul gu lo.

O fear not the bugle, though loudly it blows,
It calls but the warders that guard thy repose;
Their bows would be bended, their blades would be red,
Ere the step of a foeman drew near to thy bed.
O ho ro, i ri ri, cadul gu lo,
O ho ro, i ri ri, cadul gu lo.

O hush thee, my babie, the time soon will come
When thy sleep shall be broken by trumpet and drum;
Then hush thee, my darling, take rest while you may,
For strife comes with manhood, and waking with day.
O ho ro, i ri ri, cadul gu lo,
O ho ro, i ri ri, cadul gu lo.

THE OLIVE WOOD FIRE

When Fergus woke crying at night
I would carry him from his crib
to the rocking chair and sit holding him
before the fire of thousand-year-old olive wood.
Sometimes, for reasons I never knew
and he has forgotten, even after his bottle the big tears
would keep on rolling down his big cheeks
– the left cheek always more brilliant than the right –
and we would sit, some nights for hours, rocking
in the light eking itself out of the ancient wood,
and hold each other against the darkness,
his close behind and far away in the future,
mine I imagined all around.
One such time, fallen half-asleep myself,
I thought I heard a scream
– a flier crying out in horror
as he dropped fire on he didn't know what or whom,
or else a child thus set aflame –
and sat up alert. The olive wood fire
had burned low. In my arms lay Fergus,
fast asleep, left cheek glowing, God.

MY SON MY EXECUTIONER

My son, my executioner,
    I take you in my arms,
Quiet and small and just astir,
    And whom my body warms.

Sweet death, small son, our instrument
    Of immortality,
Your cries and hungers document
    Our bodily decay.

We twenty-five and twenty-two
    Who seemed to live forever,
Observe enduring life in you
    And start to die together.

DAUGHTER TO
FATHER

SUPERNATURAL LOVE

My father at the dictionary-stand
Touches the page to fully understand
The lamplit answer, tilting in his hand

His slowly scanning magnifying lens,
A blurry, glistening circle he suspends
Above the word "Carnation." Then he bends

So near his eyes are magnified and blurred,
One finger on the miniature word,
As if he touched a single key and heard

A distant, plucked, infinitesimal string,
"The obligation due to every thing
That's smaller than the universe." I bring

My sewing needle close enough that I
Can watch my father through the needle's eye,
As through a lens ground for a butterfly

Who peers down flower-hallways toward a room
Shadowed and fathomed as this study's gloom
Where, as a scholar bends above a tomb

To read what's buried there, he bends to pore
Over the Latin blossom. I am four,
I spill my pins and needles on the floor

Trying to stitch "Beloved" X by X.
My dangerous, bright needle's point connects
Myself illiterate to this perfect text

I cannot read. My father puzzles why
It is my habit to identify
Carnations as "Christ's flowers," knowing I

Can give no explanation but "Because."
Word-roots blossom in speechless messages
The way the thread behind my sampler does

Where following each X I awkward move
My needle through the word whose root is love.
He reads, "A pink variety of Clove,

Carnatio, the Latin, meaning flesh."
As if the bud's essential oils brush
Christ's fragrance through the room, the iron-fresh

Odor carnations have floats up to me,
A drifted, secret, bitter ecstasy,
The stems squeak in my scissors, *Child, it's me,*

He turns the page to "Clove" and reads aloud:
"The clove, a spice, dried from a flower-bud."
Then twice, as if he hasn't understood,

He reads, "From French, for *clou*, meaning a nail."
He gazes, motionless. "Meaning a nail."
The incarnation blossoms, flesh and nail,

I twist my threads like stems into a knot
And smooth "Beloved," but my needle caught
Within the threads, *Thy blood so dearly bought,*

The needle strikes my finger to the bone.
I lift my hand, it is myself I've sewn,
The flesh laid bare, the threads of blood my own,

I lift my hand in startled agony
And call upon his name, "Daddy daddy" –
My father's hand touches the injury

As lightly as he touched the page before,
Where incarnation bloomed from roots that bore
The flowers I called Christ's when I was four.

TO HER FATHER WITH SOME VERSES

Most truly honoured, and as truly dear,
If worth in me or ought I do appear,
Who can of right better demand the same
Than may your worthy self from whom it came?
The principal might yield a greater sum,
Yet handled ill, amounts but to this crumb;
My stock's so small I know not how to pay,
My bond remains in force unto this day;
Yet for part payment take this simple mite,
Where nothing's to be had, kings loose their right.
Such is my debt I may not say forgive,
But as I can, I'll pay it while I live;
Such is my bond, none can discharge but I,
Yet paying is not paid until I die.

COME HOME, FATHER!

'Tis The Song of Little Mary,
Standing at the bar-room door
While the shameful midnight revel
Rages wildly as before.

Father, dear father, come home with me now!
The clock in the steeple strikes one;
You said you were coming right home from the shop,
As soon as your day's work was done.
Our fire has gone out our house is all dark
And mother's been watching since tea, –
With poor brother Benny so sick in her arms,
And no one to help her but me. –
Come home! come home! come home! –
Please, father, dear father, come home. –

Hear the sweet voice of the child
Which the night winds repeat as they roam!
Oh who could resist this most plaintive of prayers?
"Please, father, dear father, come home."

Father, dear father, come home with me now!
The clock in the steeple strikes two;
The night has grown colder, and Benny is worse
But he has been calling for you.

Indeed he is worse Ma says he will die,
Perhaps before morning shall dawn; –
And this is the message she sent me to bring
"Come quickly, or he will be gone." –
Come home! come home! come home! –
Please, father, dear father, come home. –

Hear the sweet voice of the child
Which the night winds repeat as they roam!
Oh who could resist this most plaintive of prayers?
"Please, father, dear father, come home."

Father, dear father, come home with me now!
The clock in the steeple strikes three;
The house is so lonely the hours are so long
For poor weeping mother and me.
Yes, we are alone poor Benny is dead,
And gone with the angels of light; –
And these were the very last words that he said
"I want to kiss Papa good night." –
Come home! come home! come home! –
Please, father, dear father, come home. –

Hear the sweet voice of the child
Which the night winds repeat as they roam!
Oh who could resist this most plaintive of prayers?
"Please, father, dear father, come home."

MY FATHER AND THE FIGTREE

For other fruits my father was indifferent.
He'd point at the cherry trees and say,
"See those? I wish they were figs."
In the evenings he sat by our beds
weaving folktales like vivid little scarves.
They always involved a figtree.
Even when it didn't fit, he'd stick it in.
Once Joha was walking down the road
and he saw a figtree.
Or, he tied his camel to a figtree and went to sleep.
Or, later when they caught and arrested him,
his pockets were full of figs.

At age six I ate a dried fig and shrugged.
"That's not what I'm talking about!" he said,
"I'm talking about a fig straight from the earth —
gift of Allah! — on a branch so heavy
it touches the ground.
I'm talking about picking the largest, fattest,
        sweetest fig
in the world and putting it in my mouth."
(Here he'd stop and close his eyes.)

Years passed, we lived in many houses,
none had figtrees.
We had lima beans, zucchini, parsley, beets.
"Plant one!" my mother said,
but my father never did.
He tended garden half-heartedly, forgot to water,
let the okra get too big.
"What a dreamer he is. Look how many
things he starts and doesn't finish."

The last time he moved, I had a phone call,
my father, in Arabic, chanting a song
I'd never heard. "What's that?"
He took me out to the new yard.
There, in the middle of Dallas, Texas,
a tree with the largest, fattest,
sweetest figs in the world.
"It's a figtree song!" he said,
plucking his fruits like ripe tokens,
emblems, assurance
of a world that was always his own.

TO HER FATHER

He has gone away again.
He is out there working objects
Into holiness. Once more the house
Is empty, a phone rings like a far-off water.

She must part with something
In order to find him: her reckless
Body, its history, sleep. Even as she begins
She must give away that start:

Cannot come back to where she began.
She must be lightweight to find this river.
First the mouth. Then to look for his heart
Along the way. To head upstream toward
        the whispering,

Toward one of those narrow places
Of the earth, toward navigation.
Where rain comes down hard each afternoon,
Where other people will be. From the banks

Of the river, those who seem about to die
Salute her; their arms wave, beckon. It's unclear
What they want. She holds calm
Tightly to her sides. Repeats to herself:

Wrong is only when you know what wrong is.
She imagines he has a secret home,
A secret family. Rooms where the hum
Becomes wonderful. She thinks of the sheer

Calculation that must pass
Through him, all the symptoms
He must keep straight.
And she imagines that sometimes

He twists around, for one moment,
Sweat dripping from his face, his lip,
His shaking hands. Turns as he travels, strains
To see her through the hot light

That comes just before clouds,
Before the useless, inscrutable rain.

THE AMORER'S DAUGHTER

My father is a hard man.
When my mother couldn't give him a son,
he made the best of it; that is,
he made me into what was missing.
So I polish a breastplate until
my smudged face is reflected blue-black
and my arm is stiff as a gauntlet.

I have my father's stubborn jaw
they tell me, those boys from the village
who tease, envious of my lot.
The roughened men who come for a mending,
who bring their smooth sons to be measured,
say I have his hands, too wide for a woman.
Then I think of the beetle on the stoop
whose shell shamed the finest armor.
It scuttled away when I reached down.
With his hand.
                    I am and am not him.
Give me the dusty wings of the moths
that dared spend the night on his workbench
and I would fly – where?
Out to the hill with the shepherd?
To the mill where the miller's son
is clouded in the finest-ground flour?

This woolgathering angers my father.
He pounds music from metal,
a chorus of glow and chill, bend and stay.
I drop a helmet with a carelessness
I barely recognize and run into the yard,
into the road, tripping on my skirts.
Late afternoon, after a rain, already
the sun's low flame lights the edges
of everything. This world shines,
rings and shines, like his dream of heaven.

FOR MY FATHER

Solids and voids he balanced in the small
space of his life. His audience was bored;
would not attend, or bother to applaud.
Urban obesity claimed nearly all
his friends. His dreams grew worse, so that the air
seemed heavier each morning. Every year
winter grew more immediate, and fear
became a gravestone weight. But his despair
was something he could lift; he'd mask with grace
heart's crack and labouring strain. At last he tossed
his grief into the void. It did not come
earthward again, but stayed spinning in space.
Night was his theatre frame. Nothing was lost.
I will rest now, and eat life's honeycomb.

SNOW

Late December: my father and I
are going to New York, to the circus.
He holds me
on his shoulders in the bitter wind:
scraps of white paper
blow over the railroad ties.

My father liked
to stand like this, to hold me
so he couldn't see me.
I remember
staring straight ahead
into the world my father saw;
I was learning
to absorb its emptiness,
the heavy snow
not falling, whirling around us.

TURNING AWAY

I stand in front of my father's work;
How I look for myself and bring my story
And still it is not heard. Nothing here

To tell me what to believe. Nothing
But color, shapes he has seen,
Taken for meaning. Frames, a roomful

Of what was done without me. Once a man
And woman lay under the many stars
In a moment of one particular

Over another, which becomes the way
Of the world, which is why he left
Again and again, which is how she kept me

Until it was time. With all I have
I approach each painting. If I stare long enough
Something begins to move. If I turn away, even then

The image refuses to leave; wherever I am,
Always in the middle of all that white.

A CHINESE BOWL

Plucked from a junk shop
chipped celadon
shadow of a swallow's wing
or cast by Venetian blinds

on tinted legal pads
one summer Saturday
in 1957.
Absorbed at his big desk

my father works on briefs.
The little Royal makes
its satisfying chocks
stamping an inky nimbus

around each thick black letter
with cut-out moons for Os.
Curled up on the floor,
I'm writing too: "Bean Soup

and Rice," a play about
a poor girl in Kyoto
and the treasure-finding rabbit
who saves her home. Fluorescent

light spills cleanly down
on the Danish Modern couch
and metal cabinet
which hides no folder labelled

"blacklist" or "party business"
or "drink" or "mother's death."
I think, This is happiness,
right here, right now, these

walls striped green and gray,
shadow and sun, dust motes
stirring the still air,
and a feeling gathers, heavy

as rain about to fall,
part love, part concentration,
part inner solitude.
Where is that room, those gray-

green thin-lined
scribbled papers
littering the floor?
How did

I move so far away
just living day by day,
that now all rooms seem strange,
the years all error?
                    Bowl,

what could
I drink from you
clear green tea
or iron–bitter water

that would renew
my fallen life?

TO MY FATHER ON HIS BIRTHDAY

Amidst the days of pleasant mirth,
That throw their halo round our earth;
Amidst the tender thoughts that rise
To call bright tears to happy eyes;
Amidst the silken words that move
To syllable the names we love;
There glides no day of gentle bliss
More soothing to the heart than *this*!
No thoughts of fondness e'er appear
More fond, than those I write of here!
No name can e'er on tablet shine,
My father! more beloved than *thine*!
'Tis sweet, adown the shady past,
A lingering look of love to cast –
Back th' enchanted world to call,
That beamed around us first of all;
And walk with Memory fondly o'er
The paths where Hope had been before –
Sweet to receive the sylphic sound
That breathes in tenderness around,
Repeating to the listening ear
The names that made our childhood dear –
For parted Joy, like Echo, kind,
Will leave her dulcet voice behind,
To tell, amidst the magic air,
How oft she smiled and lingered there.

ELIZABETH BARRETT BROWNING   65

FATHER (PART 1)

My mother told me that after he left us
and we moved back to Texas,
for weeks whenever she'd take me out
I'd run and grab the pantleg
of any man I saw
(no matter if he was black or white)
shouting, "Daddy, Daddy!"

She said the white men
backed away redfaced and stiff.
The black men only laughed.

DAD, YOU RETURNED TO ME THIS MORNING

The transparent clarity
of childhood happiness,
like water.

That colorless sparkling,
tasteless but so fresh.
To drink, or ribboning over
a large stone along the brambled
bank of a river I remember.
Said to be a large wily brown
trout under there.

Two children astride me
in rumpled bed this A.M.,
and when she petted his
baby head, crooning a word
almost his name,
his eyes hooked her face,
his hands discovered applause
in halting pace:
clap (pause) clap clap!
Their mingled laughter,
the nickname again,
the merry clap–clap,
the jerking bright giggles

so free I dropped through time
and saw again the iridescence
across the belly of a trout
slipping whole in my hand
in sunlight for just long enough
to see not the usual liverish
speckling of brown but the spray
of pink, pale blue, gold-yellow
you said meant
"rainbow"
and I grasped him, wet and muscular,
smuggled in our air
for a wild moment before your
expert hand unhooked
and slipped him back.

AMATEUR FIGHTER
For my father

What's left is the tiny gold glove
hanging from his key chain. But,
before that, he had come to boxing,

as a boy, out of necessity — one more reason
to stay away from home, go late
to that cold house and dinner alone

in the dim kitchen. Perhaps he learned
just to box a stepfather, then turned
that anger into a prize at the Halifax gym.

Later, in New Orleans, there were the books
he couldn't stop reading. A scholar, his eyes
weakening. Fighting, then, a way to live

dangerously. He'd leave his front tooth out
for pictures so that I might understand
living meant suffering, loss. Really living

meant taking risks, so he swallowed
a cockroach in a bar on a dare, dreamt
of being a bullfighter. And at the gym

on Tchoupitoulas Street, he trained
his fists to pound into a bag
the fury contained in his gentle hands.

The red headgear, hiding his face,
could make me think he was someone else,
that my father was somewhere else, not here

holding his body up to pain.

BRUNNHILDE, TO HER FATHER

I do not want the curious stranger
Staring, the smell of flame brought down

To one awkward moment
When the conflagration dies enough to see

This posture of private waiting:
The place you left, done with me. What work

Keeps you from finishing, finally liable
For what you brought forth. I stayed for the storm;

I thought it between us alone. In your silence,
In the multitude of what you send my way,

The constellations are nothing
Like what I imagined. Your last look

Is what I hold in my hands like a white flower
Open as a bowl for any kind of rain.

FATHERS AND SONS

From *THE ILIAD*, BOOK VI

As he said this, Hector held out his arms
to take his baby. But the child squirmed round
on the nurse's bosom and began to wail,
terrified by his father's great war helm –
the flashing bronze, the crest with horsehair plume
tossed like a living thing at every nod.
His father began laughing, and his mother
laughed as well. Then from his handsome head
Hector lifted off his helm and bent
to place it, bright with sunlight, on the ground.
    When he had kissed his child and swung him high
to dandle him, he said this prayer: "O Zeus
and all immortals, may this child, my son,
become like me a prince among the Trojans.
Let him be strong and brave and rule in power
at Ilium; then someday men will say
'This fellow is far better than his father!'
seeing him home from war, and in his arms
the bloodstained gear of some tall warrior slain –
making his mother proud."

                 After this prayer,
into his dear wife's arms he gave his baby,
whom on her fragrant breast
she held and cherished, laughing through her tears.

From HENRY IV, PART 2

This part of his conjoins with my disease,
And helps to end me. See, sons, what things you are!
How quickly nature falls into revolt
When gold becomes her object!
For this the foolish over-careful fathers
Have broke their sleep with thoughts, their brains
    with care,
Their bones with industry; for this they have
Engrossèd and piled up the cankered heaps
Of strange-achievèd gold; for this they have
Been thoughtful to invest their sons with arts
And martial exercises; when, like the bee
Culling from every flower the virtuous sweets,
Our thighs packed with wax, our mouths with honey,
We bring it to the hive, and, like the bees,
Are murdered for our pains. This bitter taste
Yields his engrossments to the ending father.

(Act 4, Scene 5)

ALEC YEATON'S SON
Gloucester, August, 1720

The wind it wailed, the wind it moaned,
And the white caps flecked the sea;
"An' I would to God," the skipper groaned,
"I had not my boy with me!"

Snug in the stern-sheets, little John
Laughed as the scud swept by;
But the skipper's sunburnt cheeks grew wan
As he watched the wicked sky.

"Would he were at his mother's side!"
And the skipper's eyes were dim.
"Good Lord in heaven, if ill betide,
What would become of him!

"For me – my muscles are as steel,
For me let hap what may;
I might make shift upon the keel
Until the break o' day.

"But he, he is so weak and small,
So young, scarce learned to stand –
O pitying Father of us all,
I trust him in Thy hand!

"For Thou, who makest from on high
A sparrow's fall – each one! –
Surely, O Lord, thou'lt have an eye
On Alec Yeaton's son!"

Then, helm hard-port; right straight he sailed
Towards the headland light:
The wind it moaned, the wind it wailed,
And black, black fell the night.

Then burst a storm to make one quail
Though housed from winds and waves –
They who could tell about that gale
Must rise from watery graves!

Sudden it came, as sudden went;
Ere half the night was sped,
The winds were hushed, the waves were spent,
And the stars shone overhead.

Now, as the morning mist grew thin,
The folk on Gloucester shore
Saw a little figure floating in
Secure, on a broken oar!

Up rose the cry, "A wreck! a wreck!
Pull, mates, and waste no breath!" –
They knew it, though 't was but a speck
Upon the edge of death!

Long did they marvel in the town
At God his strange decree,
That let the stalwart skipper drown
And the little child go free!

MIGHTY LIKE A ROSE

Sweetest little feller,
Everybody knows;
Don't know what to call him,
But he's mighty like a rose.

Looking at his Mammy
With eyes so shiny blue,
Make you think that heaven
Is coming close to you.

DE PUERO BALBUTIENTE

Methinks 'tis pretty sport to hear a child
Rocking a word in mouth yet undefiled;
The tender racquet rudely plays the sound
Which, weakly bandied, cannot back rebound;
And the soft air the softer roof doth kiss
With a sweet dying and a pretty miss,
Which hears no answer yet from the white rank
Of teeth not risen from their coral bank.
The alphabet is searched for letters soft
To try a word before it can be wrought;
And when it slideth forth, it goes as nice
As when a man doth walk upon the ice.

TO WILLIAM SHELLEY

I

The billows on the beach are leaping around it,
  The bark is weak and frail,
The sea looks black, and the clouds that bound it
  Darkly strew the gale.
Come with me, thou delightful child,
Come with me, though the wave is wild,
And the winds are loose, we must not stay,
Or the slaves of the law may rend thee away.

II

They have taken thy brother and sister dear,
  They have made them unfit for thee;
They have withered the smile and dried the tear
  Which should have been sacred to me.
To a blighting faith and a cause of crime
They have bound them slaves in youthly prime,
And they will curse my name and thee
Because we fearless are and free.

III

Come thou, beloved as thou art;
  Another sleepeth still
Near thy sweet mother's anxious heart,
  Which thou with joy shalt fill,

With fairest smiles of wonder thrown
On that which is indeed our own,
And which in distant lands will be
The dearest playmate unto thee.

IV

Fear not the tyrants will rule for ever,
   Or the priests of the evil faith;
They stand on the brink of that raging river,
   Whose waves they have tainted with death.
It is fed from the depths of a thousand dells,
Around them it foams and rages and swells;
And their swords and their sceptres I floating see,
Like wrecks on the surge of eternity.

V

Rest, rest, and shriek not, thou gentle child!
   The rocking of the boat thou fearest,
And the cold spray and the clamour wild? –
   There, sit between us two, thou dearest –
Me and thy mother – well we know
The storm at which thou tremblest so,
With all its dark and hungry graves,
Less cruel than the savage slaves
Who hunt us o'er these sheltering waves.

VI

This hour will in thy memory
    Be a dream of days forgotten long.
We soon shall dwell by the azure sea
Of serene and golden Italy,
Or Greece, the Mother of the free;
    And I will teach thine infant tongue
To call upon those heroes old
In their own language, and will mould
Thy growing spirit in the flame
Of Grecian lore, that by such name
A patriot's birthright thou mayst claim!

"CHILD, WHEN THEY SAY THAT OTHERS"
From *Comparisons*

Child, when they say that others
   Have been or are like you,
Babes fit to be your brothers,
   Sweet human drops of dew,
Bright fruit of mortal mothers,
   What should one say or do?

We know the thought is treason,
   We feel the dream absurd;
A claim rebuked of reason,
   That withers at a word:
For never shone the season
   That bore so blithe a bird.

Some smiles may seem as merry,
   Some glances gleam as wise,
From lips as like a cherry
   And scarce less gracious eyes;
Eyes browner than a berry,
   Lips red as morning's rise.

But never yet rang laughter
    So sweet in gladdened ears
Through wall and floor and rafter
    As all this household bears
And rings response thereafter
    Till cloudiest weather clears.

The dawn were not more cheerless
    With neither light nor dew
Than we without the fearless
    Clear laugh that thrills us through:
If ever child stood peerless,
    Love knows that child is you.

ANECDOTE FOR FATHERS

I have a boy of five years old;
His face is fair and fresh to see;
His limbs are cast in beauty's mold
And dearly he loves me.

One morn we strolled on our dry walk,
Or quiet home all full in view,
And held such intermitted talk
As we are wont to do.

My thoughts on former pleasures ran;
I thought of Kilve's delightful shore,
Our pleasant home when spring began,
A long, long year before.

A day it was when I could bear
Some fond regrets to entertain;
With so much happiness to spare,
I could not feel a pain.

The green earth echoed to the feet
Of lambs that bounded through the glade,
From shade to sunshine, and as fleet
From sunshine back to shade.

Birds warbled round me – and each trace
Of inward sadness had its charm;
Kilve, thought I, was a favoured place,
And so is Liswyn farm.

My boy beside me tripped, so slim
And graceful in his rustic dress!
And, as we talked, I questioned him,
In very idleness.

"Now tell me, had you rather be,"
I said, and took him by the arm,
"On Kilve's smooth shore, by the green sea,
Or here at Liswyn farm?"

In careless mood he looked at me,
While still I held him by the arm,
And said, "At Kilve I'd rather be
Than here at Liswyn farm."

"Now, little Edward, say why so:
My little Edward, tell me why." –
"I cannot tell, I do not know." –
"Why, this is strange," said I;

"For, here are woods, hills smooth and warm:
There surely must one reason be
Why you would change sweet Liswyn farm
For Kilve by the green sea."

At this, my boy hung down his head,
He blushed with shame, nor made reply;
And three times to the child I said,
"Why, Edward, tell me why?"

His head he raised — there was in sight,
It caught his eye, he saw it plain —
Upon the house-top, glittering bright,
A broad and gilded vane.

Then did the boy his tongue unlock,
And eased his mind with this reply:
"At Kilve there was no weather-cock;
And that's the reaon why."

O dearest, dearest boy! my heart
For better lore would seldom yearn,
Could I but teach the hundredth part
Of what from thee I learn.

THE TOYS

My little son, who looked from thoughtful eyes
And moved and spoke in quiet grown-up wise,
Having my law the seventh time disobeyed,
I struck him, and dismissed
With hard words and unkissed,
His mother, who was patient, being dead.
Then, fearing lest his grief should hinder sleep,
I visited his bed,
But found him slumbering deep,
With darkened eyelids, and their lashes yet
From his late sobbing wet.
And I, with moan,
Kissing away his tears, left others of my own;
For, on a table drawn beside his head,
He had put, within his reach,
A box of counters and a red-veined stone,
A piece of glass abraded by the beach
And six or seven shells,
A bottle with bluebells
And two French copper coins, ranged there with
    careful art,
To comfort his sad heart.
So when that night I prayed
To God, I wept, and said:
Ah, when at last we lie with tranced breath,

Not vexing Thee in death,
And Thou rememberest of what toys
We made our joys,
How weakly understood,
Thy great commanded good,
Then, fatherly not less
Than I whom Thou hast moulded from the clay,
Thou'lt leave Thy wrath, and say,
"I will be sorry for their childishness."

COVENTRY PATMORE

A PARENTAL ODE TO MY SON, AGED
THREE YEARS AND FIVE MONTHS

    Thou happy, happy elf!
(But stop. – first let me kiss away that tear) –
    Thou tiny image of myself!
(My love, he's poking peas into his ear!)
    Thou merry, laughing sprite!
    With spirits feather-light,
Untouched by sorrow, and unsoiled by sin –
(Good heavens! the child is swallowing a pin!)

    Thou little tricksy Puck!
With antic toys so funnily bestuck,
Light as the singing bird that wings the air –
(The door! the door! he'll tumble down the stair!)
    Thou darling of thy sire!
(Why, Jane, he'll set his pinafore a-fire!)
    Thou imp of mirth and joy!
In Love's dear chain so strong and bright a link,
Thou idol of thy parents – (Drat the boy!
    There goes my ink!)

    Thou cherub – but of earth;
Fit playfellow for Fays, by moonlight pale.
    In harmless sport and mirth,
(That dog will bite him if he pulls its tail!)

Thou human humming-bee extracting honey
From ev'ry blossom in the world that blows,
    Singing in Youth's Elysium ever sunny,
(Another tumble! – that's his precious nose!)
    Thy father's pride and hope!
(He'll break the mirror with that skipping-rope!)
With pure heart newly stamped from Nature's mint –
    (Where did he learn that squint?)

    Thou young domestic dove!
(He'll have that jug off, with another shove!)
    Dear nursling of the hymeneal nest!
        (Are those torn clothes his best!)
    Little epitome of man!
(He'll climb upon the table, that's his plan!)
Touched with the beauteous tints of dawning life –
        (He's got a knife!)

    Thou enviable being!
No storms, no clouds, in thy blue sky foreseeing,
        Play on, play on.
        My elfin John!
Toss the light ball – bestride the stick –
(I knew so many cakes would make him sick!)
With fancies buoyant as the thistle down,
Prompting the face grotesque, and antic brisk,
        With many a lamb-like frisk,
(He's got the scissors, snipping at your gown!)

Thou pretty opening rose!
(Go to your mother, child, and wipe your nose!)
Balmy, and breathing music like the South,
(He really brings my heart into my mouth!)
Fresh as the morn, and brilliant as its star –
(I wish that window had an iron bar!)
Bold as the hawk, yet gentle as the dove –
    (I tell you what my love,
I cannot write, unless he's sent above!)

THE CHILD IS FATHER TO THE MAN

"The child is father to the man."
How can he be? The words are wild.
Suck any sense from that who can:
"The child is father to the man."
No; what the poet did write ran,
"The man is father to the child."
"The child is father to the man!"
How can he be? The words are wild.

DUST AS WE ARE

My post-war father was so silent
He seemed to be listening. I eavesdropped
On the hot line. His lonely sittings
Mangled me, in secret – like TV
Watched too long, my nerves lasered.
Then, an after image of the incessant
Mowing passage of machine-gun effects,
What it filled a trench with. And his laugh
(How had that survived – so nearly intact?)
Twitched the curtain never quite deftly enough
Over the hospital wards
Crowded with his (photographed) shock-eyed pals.

I had to use up a lot of spirit
Getting over it. I was helping him.
I was his supplementary convalescent.
He took up his pre-war *joie de vivre*.
But his displays of muscular definition
Were a bleached montage – lit landscapes:
Swampquakes of the slime of puddled soldiers
Where bones and bits of equipment
Showered from every shell-burst.
                              Naked men
Slithered staring where their mothers and sisters
Would never have to meet their eyes, or see
Exactly how they sprawled and were trodden.

So he had been salvaged and washed.
His muscles very white – marble white.
He had been heavily killed. But we had revived him.
Now he taught us a silence like prayer.
There he sat, killed but alive – so long
As we were very careful. I divined,
With a comb,
Under his wavy, golden hair, as I combed it,
The fragility of skull. And I filled
With his knowledge.
                    After mother's milk
This was the soul's food. A soap-smell spectre
Of the massacre of innocents. So the soul grew.
A strange thing, with rickets – a hyena.
No singing – that kind of laughter.

FOLLOWER

My father worked with a horse-plough,
His shoulders globed like a full sail strung
Between the shafts and the furrow.
The horses strained at his clicking tongue.

An expert. He would set the wing
And fit the bright steel-pointed sock.
The sod rolled over without breaking.
At the headrig, with a single pluck

Of reins, the sweating team turned round
And back into the land. His eye
Narrowed and angled at the ground,
Mapping the furrow exactly.

I stumbled in his hobnailed wake,
Fell sometimes on the polished sod;
Sometimes he rode me on his back
Dipping and rising to his plod.

I wanted to grow up and plough,
To close one eye, stiffen my arm.
All I ever did was follow
In his broad shadow round the farm.

I was a nuisance, tripping, falling,
Yapping always. But today
It is my father who keeps stumbling
Behind me, and will not go away.

DIGGING

Between my finger and my thumb
The squat pen rests; snug as a gun.

Under my window, a clean rasping sound
When the spade sinks into gravelly ground:
My father, digging. I look down

Till his straining rump among the flowerbeds
Bends low, comes up twenty years away
Stooping in rhythm through potato drills
Where he was digging.

The coarse boot nestled on the lug, the shaft
Against the inside knee was levered firmly.
He rooted out tall tops, buried the bright edge deep
To scatter new potatoes that we picked,
Loving their cool hardness in our hands.

By God, the old man could handle a spade.
Just like his old man.

My grandfather cut more turf in a day
Than any other man on Toner's bog.
Once I carried him milk in a bottle
Corked sloppily with paper. He straightened up

To drink it, then fell to right away
Nicking and slicing neatly, heaving sods
Over his shoulder, going down and down
For the good turf. Digging.

The cold smell of potato mould, the squelch and slap
Of soggy peat, the curt cuts of an edge
Through living roots awaken in my head.
But I've no spade to follow men like them.

Between my finger and my thumb
The squat pen rests.
I'll dig with it.

THE NOD

Saturday evenings we would stand in line
In Loudan's butcher shop. Red beef, white string,
Brown paper ripped straight off for parcelling
Along the counter edge. Rib roast and shin
Plonked down, wrapped up, and bow-tied neat
    and clean
But seeping blood. Like dead weight in a sling,
Heavier far than I had been expecting
While my father shelled out for it, coin by coin.

Saturday evenings too the local B-Men,
Unbuttoned but on duty, thronged the town,
Neighbours with guns, parading up and down,
Some nodding at my father almost past him
As if deliberately they'd aimed and missed him
Or couldn't seem to place him, not just then.

AFTER MAKING LOVE
WE HEAR FOOTSTEPS

For I can snore like a bullhorn
or play loud music
or sit up talking with any reasonably sober Irishman
and Fergus will only sink deeper
into his dreamless sleep, which goes by all in one flash,
but let there be that heavy breathing
or a stifled come-cry anywhere in the house
and he will wrench himself awake
and make for it on the run – as now, we lie together,
after making love, quiet, touching along the length of
        our bodies,
familiar touch of the long-married,
and he appears – in his baseball pajamas, it happens,
the neck opening so small
he has to screw them on, which one day may make
        him wonder
about the mental capacity of baseball players –
and says, "Are you loving and snuggling? May I join?"
He flops down between us and hugs us and snuggles
        himself to sleep,
his face gleaming with satisfaction at being this
        very child.

In the half darkness we look at each other
and smile
and touch arms across his little, startlingly muscled
    body –
this one whom habit of memory propels to the ground
    of his making,
sleeper only the mortal sounds can sing awake,
this blessing love gives again into our arms.

SEPTEMBER, THE FIRST DAY OF SCHOOL

I

My child and I hold hands on the way to school,
And when I leave him at the first-grade door
He cries a little but is brave; he does
Let go. My selfish tears remind me how
I cried before that door a life ago.
I may have had a hard time letting go.

Each fall the children must endure together
What every child also endures alone:
Learning the alphabet, the integers,
Three dozen bits and pieces of a stuff
So arbitrary, so peremptory
That worlds invisible and visible

Bow down before it, as in Joseph's dream
The sheaves bowed down and then the stars
     bowed down
Before the dreaming of a little boy.
That dream got him such hatred of his brothers
As cost the greater part of life to mend,
And yet great kindness came of it in the end.

II

A school is where they grind the grain of thought,
And grind the children who must mind the thought.
It may be those two grindings are but one,
As from the alphabet come Shakespeare's Plays,
As from the integers comes Euler's Law,
As from the whole, inseparably, the lives,

The shrunken lives that have not been set free
By law or by poetic phantasy.
But may they be. My child has disappeared
Behind the schoolroom door. And should I live
To see his coming forth, a life away,
I know my hope, but do not know its form

Nor hope to know it. May the fathers he finds
Among his teachers have a care of him
More than his father could. How that will look
I do not know, I do not need to know.
Even our tears belong to ritual.
But may great kindness come of it in the end.

From DREAM SONGS
(no. 241)

Father being the loneliest word in the one language
and a word only, a fraction of sun & guns
'way 'way ago,
on a hillside, under rain, maneuvers, once,
at big dawn. My field-glasses surpass – he sang –
yours.

Wicked & powerful, shy Henry lifted his head with
    an offering.
Boots greeted him & it.
I raced into the bank,
my bank, after two years, with healthy cheques
& nobody seem to know me: was I ex-:
like Daddy??

O. O . . . I can't help feel I lift' the strain,
toward bottom. Games is somewhat too, but yet
certains improve
as if upon their only. We grinned wif wuv
for that which each of else was master of.
Christen the fallen.

JOHN BERRYMAN   107

LISTENING

My father could hear a little animal step,
or a moth in the dark against the screen,
and every far sound called the listening out
into places where the rest of us had never been.

More spoke to him from the soft wild night
than came to our porch for us on the wind;
we would watch him look up and his face go keen
till the walls of the world flared, widened.

My father heard so much that we still stand
inviting the quiet by turning the face,
waiting for a time when something in the night
will touch us too from that other place.

INSCRIPTION FOR MY LITTLE SON'S SILVER PLATE

When thou dost eat from off this plate,
I charge thee be thou temperate;
Unto thine elders at the board
Do thou sweet reverence accord;
And, though to dignity inclined,
Unto the serving-folk be kind;
Be ever mindful of the poor,
Nor turn them hungry from the door;
And unto God, for health and food
And all that in thy life is good,
Give thou thy heart in gratitude.

EUGENE FIELD

ELEGY FOR MY FATHER,
WHO IS NOT DEAD

One day I'll lift the telephone
and be told my father's dead. He's ready.
In the sureness of his faith, he talks
about the world beyond this world
as though his reservations have
been made. I think he wants to go,
a little bit — a new desire
to travel building up, an itch
to see fresh worlds. Or older ones.
He thinks that when I follow him
he'll wrap me in his arms and laugh,
the way he did when I arrived
on earth. I do not think he's right.
He's ready. I am not. I can't
just say good-bye as cheerfully
as if he were embarking on a trip
to make my later trip go well.
I see myself on deck, convinced
his ship's gone down, while he's convinced
I'll see him standing on the dock
and waving, shouting, *Welcome back*.

THE BRANCH

The artist in my father transformed the diagonal
Crack across the mirror on our bathroom cabinet
Into a branch: that was his way of mending things,
A streak of brown paint, dabs of green, an accident
That sprouted leaves,
                            awakening the child in me
To the funny faces he pulls when he is shaving.
He wears a vest, white buttons at his collarbone.
The two halves of my father's face are joining up.
His soapy nostrils disappear among the leaves.

FATHER IN THE LIBRARY
From *The World*

A high forehead, and above it tousled hair
On which a ray of sun falls from the window.
And so father wears a bright fluffy crown
When he spreads before him a huge book.

His gown is patterned like that of a wizard.
Softly, he murmurs his incantations.
Only he whom God instructs in magic
Will learn what wonders are hidden in this book.

FATHER'S INCANTATIONS
From *The World*

O sweet master, with how much peace
Your serene wisdom fills the heart!
I love you, I am in your power
Even though I will never see your face.

Your ashes have long been scattered,
Your sins and follies no one remembers.
And for ages you will remain perfect
Like your book drawn by thought from nothingness.

You knew bitterness and you knew doubt
But the memory of your faults has vanished.
And I know why I cherish you today:
Men are small but their works are great.

MY SON, MY SON, MY HEAD, MY HEAD

My son, my son, my head, my head,
In this train, I pass
Through alien landscape, reading of Auschwitz
And learning about the difference
Between "to leave" and "not to remain."

My son, my head, my head, my son,
The roads are wet like a drowned woman
Pulled out of the river at dawn
After a wild search with crazy lights.
Now silence:
Shining dead body.

My head, my head, my son, my son!
The inability to define your pain precisely
Impedes the doctors from diagnosing an illness.
It means we can never
Really love.

ODYSSEUS TO TELEMACHUS

My dear Telemachus,
    The Trojan War
is over now; I don't recall who won it.
The Greeks, no doubt, for only they would leave
so many dead so far from their own homeland.
But still, my homeward way has proved too long.
While we were wasting time there, old Poseidon,
it almost seems, stretched and extended space.

I don't know where I am or what this place
can be. It would appear some filthy island,
with bushes, buildings, and great grunting pigs.
A garden choked with weeds; some queen or other.
Grass and huge stones . . . Telemachus, my son!
To a wanderer the faces of all islands
resemble one another. And the mind
trips, numbering waves; eyes, sore from sea horizons,
run; and the flesh of water stuffs the ears.
I can't remember how the war came out;
even how old you are – I can't remember.

Grow up, then, my Telemachus, grow strong.
Only the gods know if we'll see each other
again. You've long since ceased to be that babe
before whom I reined in the plowing bullocks.

Had it not been for Palamedes' trick
we two would still be living in one household.
But maybe he was right; away from me
you are quite safe from all Oedipal passions,
and your dreams, my Telemachus, are blameless.

TELEMACHUS' FANTASY

Sometimes I wonder about my father's
years on those islands: why
was he so attractive
to women? He was in straits then, I suppose
desperate. I believe
women like to see a man
still whole, still standing, but
about to go to pieces: such
disintegration reminds them
of passion. I think of them as living
their whole lives
completely undressed. It must have
dazzled him, I think, women
so much younger than he was
evidently wild for him, ready
to do anything he wished. Is it
fortunate to encounter circumstances
so responsive to one's own will, to live
so many years
unquestioned, unthwarted? One
would have to believe oneself
entirely good or worthy. I
suppose in time either
one becomes a monster or
the beloved sees what one is. I never

wish for my father's life
nor have I any idea
what he sacrificed
to survive that moment. Less dangerous
to believe he was drawn to them
and so stayed
to see who they were. I think, though,
as an imaginative man
to some extent he
became who they were.

HAMLET

The buzz subsides. I have come on stage.
Leaning in an open door
I try to detect from the echo
What the future has in store.

A thousand opera-glasses level
The dark, point-blank, at me.
Abba, Father, if it be possible
Let this cup pass from me.

I love your preordained design
And am ready to play this role.
For this once let me go.

BORIS PASTERNAK
TRANSLATED BY JON STALLWORTHY AND
PETER FRANCE

THE CHANGELING

A man had a son who was an anvil. And then sometimes he was an automobile tire.

I do wish you would sit still, said the father.

Sometimes his son was a rock.

I realize that you have quite lost boundary, where no excess seems excessive, nor to where poverty roots hunger to need. But should you allow time to embrace you to its bosom of dust, that velvet sleep, then were you served even beyond your need; and desire in sate was properly spilling from its borders, said the father.

Then his son became the corner of a room.

Don't don't, cried the father.

And then his son became a floorboard.

Don't don't, the moon falls there and curdles your wits into the grain of the wood, cried the father.

What shall I do? screamed his son.

Sit until time embraces you into the bosom of its velvet quiet, cried the father.

Like this? cried his son as his son became dust.

Ah, that is more pleasant, and speaks well of him, who having required much in his neglect of proper choice, turns now, on good advice, to a more advantageous social stance, said the father.

But then his son became his father.

Behold, the son is become as one of us, said the father.

His son said, behold, the son is become as one of us.

Will you stop repeating me, screamed the father.

Will you stop repeating me, screamed his son.

Oh well, I suppose imitation is the sincerest form of flattery, sighed the father.

Oh well, I suppose imitation is the sincerest form of flattery, sighed his son.

PHOTOGRAPH OF MY FATHER
IN HIS TWENTY-SECOND YEAR

October. Here in this dank, unfamiliar kitchen
I study my father's embarrassed young man's face.
Sheepish grin, he holds in one hand a string
Of spiny yellow perch, in the other
A bottle of Carlsbad beer.

In jeans and denim shirt, he leans
Against the front fender of a Ford *circa* 1934.
He would like to pose bluff and hearty for his posterity,
Wear his old hat cocked over his ear, stick out his
      tongue...
All his life my father wanted to be bold.

But the eyes gave him away, and the hands
That limply offer a string of dead perch
And the bottle of beer. Father, I loved you,
Yet how can I say thank you, I who cannot hold my
      liquor either
And do not even know the places to fish?

THE PAST

along many empty streets my heart is sustained
by the beauty of the brownstones
after they are torn down. I still don't know
whether to trust the dead branches,
to rely on broken glass on the sidewalk
made nearly whole again by what it once made visible:
pink and yellow sugary window shades transcending
rotten tin gutters, a passing brown Desoto,
the hand of a young girl in a bright sleeve
dangling from the car window. It is like
my father is alive again, sporting
a well trimmed mustache, his Saturday-night suit.
he is standing in wing-tips in his kitchenette,
sipping tea, scratching tomorrow's beard, scruffy
with romance and sorrow. The light is fading
but I must see him to believe
in the smell of lilacs from across the river.
it is time I put my faith in the past.
it is time I opened the door to his apartment
in 242 Dumont Avenue and confessed everything.

GIFTS

I

I stood in the tunnel warehouse
holding hands with my brother and Dad,
with our Red Flyer wagon that the Goodfellows left.
We came for potatoes, salt pork, beans, and flour.
The lines were long, but we had to stay. Strangers
waited with us, against the flush of winter.

II

Lunch at the Book Cadillac, second basement.
Our uncle worked in the Kay Danzer Flower Shop.
He took roses to the stadium ticket window.
We got to see the Tigers play the Yankees.
Greenberg hit one out onto Cherry Street.

III

I had a report due in Social Science.
Finished it while Mom did the dishes.
I washed my safety-patrol belt every Monday.
Mr. Loving expected them to be spotless.
I brushed, scrubbed, and soaked it.
Mom suggested table salt. It glowed.

IV

Mom told Dad I wanted to go to college.
We didn't have money for school.
Dad pulled out the blue pin-striped suit
that he saved for special good times,
looked it over, fondled the jacket, took the suit
to Lewis's, the pawnshop on Gratiot.

MY FATHER PAINTS THE SUMMER

A smoky rain riddles the ocean plains,
Rings on the beaches' stones, stomps in the swales,
Batters the panes
Of the shore hotel, and the hoped-for summer chills
    and fails.
The summer people sigh,
"Is this July?"

They talk by the lobby fire but no one hears
For the thrum of the rain. In the dim and sounding halls,
Din at the ears,
Dark at the eyes well in the head, and the ping-pong balls
Scatter their hollow knocks
Like crazy clocks.

But up in his room by artificial light
My father paints the summer, and his brush
Tricks into sight
The prosperous sleep, the girdling stir and clear
    steep hush
Of a summer never seen,
A granted green.

Summer, luxuriant Sahara, the orchard spray
Gales in the Eden trees, the knight again
Can cast away
His burning mail, Rome is at Anzio: but the rain
For the ping-pong's optative bop
Will never stop.

Caught Summer is always an imagined time.
Time gave it, yes, but time out of any mind.
There must be prime
In the heart to beget that season, to reach past
        rain and find
Riding the palest days
Its perfect blaze.

FATHER TO
DAUGHTER

From KING LEAR

Winter's not gone yet, if the wild geese fly that way.
    Fathers that wear rags
      Do make their children blind,
    But fathers that bear bags
      Shall see their children kind.
    Fortune, that arrant whore,
      Ne'er turns the key to th'poor.
But for all this, thou shalt have as many dolours for
    thy daughters
as thou canst tell in a year.

TO A CHILD

My fairest child, I have no song to sing thee;
No lark could pipe in skies so dull and grey;
Yet, if thou wilt, one lesson I will give thee
For every day.

Be good, sweet maid, and let who can be clever;
Do lovely things, not dream them, all day long;
And so make Life, Death, and that vast For Ever
One grand sweet song.

ON MY FIRST DAUGHTER

Here lies to each her parents' ruth,
Mary, the daughter of their youth:
Yet, all Heaven's gifts being heaven's due,
It makes the father less to rue.
At six months' end she parted hence
With safety of her innocence;
Whose soul heaven's queen (whose name she bears),
In comfort of her mother's tears,
Hath placed amongst her virgin train:
Where, while that severed doth remain,
This grave partakes the fleshly birth;
Which cover lightly, gentle earth.

BEN·JONSON   133

A POET'S WELCOME TO HIS
LOVE-BEGOTTEN DAUGHTER

Thou's welcome, wean! Mishanter fa' me,
If thoughts of thee, or yet thy Mamie,
Shall ever daunton me or awe me
   My bonie lady;
Or if I blush when thou shalt ca' me
   Tyta, or daddie.

What tho they ca' me fornicator,
An tease my name in kintra clatter,
The mair they talk, I'm ken'd the better,
   E'en let them clash!
An auld wife's tongue's a feckless matter
   To gie ane fash.

Welcome my bonie, sweet, wee dochter!
Tho ye come here a wee unsought for,
And tho your comin I hae fought for,
   Baith Kirk and Queir;
Yet, by my faith, ye're no unwrought for,
   That I shall swear!

Sweet fruit o monie a merry dint,
My funny toil is no a' tint,
Tho thou cam to the warl' asklent,

Which fools may scoff at,
In my last plack your part's be in't
    The better half o't.

Tho I should be the waur bestead,
Thou's be as braw and bienly clad,
And thy young years as nicely bred
    Wi education,
As onie brat o wedlock's bed,
    In a' thy station.

Lord grant that thou may ay inherit
Thy mither's looks an gracefu merit,
An thy poor, worthless daddie's spirit.
    Without his failins!
Twill please me mair to see thee heir it,
    Than stocket mailins.

For if thou be what I wad hae thee,
An tak the counsel I shall gie thee,
I'll never rue my trouble wi thee,
    The cost nor shame o't,
But be a loving father to thee,
And brag the name o't.

ROBERT BURNS   135

TO IANTHE

I love thee, Baby! For thine own sweet sake;
    Those azure eyes, that faintly dimpled cheek.
    Thy tender frame, so eloquently weak,
    Love in the sternest heart of hate might wake;
But more when o'er thy fitful slumber bending
    Thy mother folds thee to her wakeful heart,
    Whilst love and pity, in her glances bending,
    All that thy passive eyes can feel impart:
More, when some feeble lineaments of her,
    Who bore thy weight beneath her spotless bosom,
    As with deep love I read thy face, recur! —
More dear art thou, O fair and fragile blossom;
    Dearest when most thy tender traits express
    The image of thy mother's loveliness.

FOR JESSICA, MY DAUGHTER

Tonight I walked,
lost in my own meditation,
and was afraid,
not of the labyrinth
that I have made of love and self
but of the dark and faraway.
I walked, hearing the wind in the trees,
feeling the cold against my skin,
but what I dwelled on
were the stars blazing
in the immense arc of sky.

Jessica, it is so much easier
to think of our lives,
as we move under the brief luster of leaves,
loving what we have,
than to think of how it is
such small beings as we
travel in the dark
with no visible way
or end in sight.

Yet there were times I remember
under the same sky
when the body's bones became light

and the wound of the skull
opened to receive
the cold rays of the cosmos,
and were, for an instant,
themselves the cosmos,
there were times when I could believe
we were the children of stars
and our words were made of the same
dust that flames in space,
times when I could feel in the lightness of breath
the weight of a whole day
come to rest.

But tonight
it is different.
Afraid of the dark
in which we drift or vanish altogether,
I imagine a light
that would not let us stray too far apart,
a secret moon or mirror,
a sheet of paper,
something you could carry
in the dark
when I am away.

TO MY DAUGHTER

Bright clasp of her whole hand around my finger,
My daughter, as we walk together now.
All my life I'll feel a ring invisibly
Circle this bone with shining: when she is grown
Far from today as her eyes are far already.

SARA IN HER FATHER'S ARMS

Cell by cell the baby made herself, the cells
Made cells. That is to say
The baby is made largely of milk. Lying in her
    father's arms, the little seed eyes
Moving, trying to see, smiling for us
To see, she will make a household
To her need of these rooms – Sara, little seed,
Little violent, diligent seed. Come let us look
    at the world
Glittering: this seed will speak,
Max, words! There will be no other words in the world
But those our children speak. What will she make
    of a world
Do you suppose, Max, of which she is made.

FULL MOON AND LITTLE FRIEDA

A cool small evening shrunk to a dog bark
    and the clank of a bucket –

And you listening.
A spider's web, tense for the dew's touch.
A pail lifted, still and brimming – mirror
To tempt a first star to a tremor.

Cows are going home in the lane there, looping the
    hedges with their warm wreaths of breath –
A dark river of blood, many boulders,
Balancing unspilled milk.

"Moon!" you cry suddenly, "Moon! Moon!"

The moon has stepped back like an artist
    gazing amazed at a work

That points at him amazed.

THE WRITER

In her room at the prow of the house
Where light breaks, and the windows are tossed
        with linden,
My daughter is writing a story.

I pause in the stairwell, hearing
From her shut door a commotion of typewriter-keys
Like a chain hauled over a gunwale.

Young as she is, the stuff
Of her life is a great cargo, and some of it heavy:
I wish her a lucky passage.

But now it is she who pauses,
As if to reject my thought and its easy figure.
A stillness greatens, in which

The whole house seems to be thinking,
And then she is at it again with a bunched clamor
Of strokes, and again is silent.

I remember the dazed starling
Which was trapped in that very room, two years ago;
How we stole in, lifted a sash

And retreated, not to affright it;
And how for a helpless hour, through the crack
    of the door,
We watched the sleek, wild, dark

And iridescent creature
Batter against the brilliance, drop like a glove
To the hard floor, or the desk-top,

And wait then, humped and bloody,
For the wits to try it again; and how our spirits
Rose when, suddenly sure,

It lifted off from a chair-back,
Beating a smooth course for the right window
And clearing the sill of the world.

It is always a matter, my darling,
Of life or death, as I had forgotten. I wish
What I wished you before, but harder.

A PRAYER FOR MY DAUGHTER

Once more the storm is howling, and half hid
Under this cradle-hood and coverlid
My child sleeps on. There is no obstacle
But Gregory's wood and one bare hill
Whereby the haystack- and roof-levelling wind,
Bred on the Atlantic, can be stayed;
And for an hour I have walked and prayed
Because of the great gloom that is in my mind.

I have walked and prayed for this young child an hour
And heard the sea-wind scream upon the tower,
And under the arches of the bridge, and scream
In the elms above the flooded stream;
Imagining in excited reverie
That the future years had come,
Dancing to a frenzied drum,
Out of the murderous innocence of the sea.

May she be granted beauty and yet not
Beauty to make a stranger's eye distraught,
Or hers before a looking-glass, for such,
Being made beautiful overmuch,
Consider beauty a sufficient end,
Lose natural kindness and maybe
The heart-revealing intimacy
That chooses right, and never find a friend.

Helen being chosen found life flat and dull
And later had much trouble from a fool,
While that great Queen, that rose out of the spray,
Being fatherless could have her way
Yet chose a bandy-leggèd smith for man.
It's certain that fine women eat
A crazy salad with their meat
Whereby the Horn of Plenty is undone.

In courtesy I'd have her chiefly learned;
Hearts are not had as a gift but hearts are earned
By those that are not entirely beautiful;
Yet many, that have played the fool
For beauty's very self, has charm made wise,
And many a poor man that has roved,
Loved and thought himself beloved,
From a glad kindness cannot take his eyes.

May she become a flourishing hidden tree
That all her thoughts may like the linnet be,
And have no business but dispensing round
Their magnanimities of sound,
Nor but in merriment begin a chase,
Nor but in merriment a quarrel.
O may she live like some green laurel
Rooted in one dear perpetual place.

My mind, because the minds that I have loved,
The sort of beauty that I have approved,
Prosper but little, has dried up of late,
Yet knows that to be choked with hate
May well be of all evil chances chief.
If there's no hatred in a mind
Assault and battery of the wind
Can never tear the linnet from the leaf.

An intellectual hatred is the worst,
So let her think opinions are accursed.
Have I not seen the loveliest woman born
Out of the mouth of Plenty's horn,
Because of her opinionated mind
Barter that horn and every good
By quiet natures understood
For an old bellows full of angry wind?

Considering that, all hatred driven hence,
The soul recovers radical innocence
And learns at last that it is self-delighting,
Self-appeasing, self-affrighting,
And that its own sweet will is Heaven's will;
She can, though every face should scowl
And every windy quarter howl
Or every bellows burst, be happy still.

And may her bridegroom bring her to a house
Where all's accustomed, ceremonious;
For arrogance and hatred are the wares
Peddled in the thoroughfares.
How but in custom and in ceremony
Are innocence and beauty born?
Ceremony's a name for the rich horn,
And custom for the spreading laurel tree.

W. B. YEATS

GRANDFATHERS

FOR GRANDFATHER

How far north are you by now?
– But I'm almost close enough to see you:
under the North Star,
stocky, broadbacked, & determined,
trudging on splaying snowshoes
over the snow's hard, brilliant, curdled crust . . .
Aurora Borealis burns in silence.
Streamers of red, of purple,
fleck with color your bald head.
Where is your sealskin cap with ear-lugs?
That old fur coat with the black frogs?
You'll catch your death again.

If I should overtake you, kiss your cheek,
its silver stubble would feel like hoar-frost
and your old-fashioned, walrus moustache
be hung with icicles.

Creak, creak . . . frozen thongs and creaking snow.
These drifts are endless, I think; as far as the Pole
they hold no shadows but their own, and ours.
Grandfather, please stop! I haven't been this cold
    in years.

GRANDFATHER IN THE OLD
MEN'S HOME

Gentle at last, and as clean as ever,
He did not even need drink any more,
And his good sons unbent and brought him
Tobacco to chew, both times when they came
To be satisfied he was well cared for.
And he smiled all the time to remember
Grandmother, his wife, wearing the true faith
Like an iron nightgown, yet brought to birth
Seven times and raising the family
Through her needle's eye while he got away
Down the green river, finding directions
For boats. And himself coming home sometimes
Well-heeled but blind drunk, to hide all the bread
And shoot holes in the bucket while he made
His daughters pump. Still smiled as kindly in
His sleep beside the other clean old men
To see Grandmother, every night the same,
Huge in her age, with her thumbed-down mouth, come
Hating the river, filling with her stare
His gliding dream, while he turned to water,
While the children they both had begotten,
With old faces now, but themselves shrunken
To child-size again, stood ranged at her side,
Beating their little Bibles till he died.

GRANDFATHER'S LOVE

They said he sent his love to me,
They wouldn't put it in my hand,
And when I asked them where it was
They said I couldn't understand.

I thought they must have hidden it,
I hunted for it all the day,
And when I told them so at night
They smiled and turned their heads away.

They say that love is something kind,
That I can never see or touch.
I wish he'd sent me something else,
I like his cough-drops twice as much.

CLIMBING MY GRANDFATHER

I decide to do it free, without a rope or net.
First, the old brogues, dusty and cracked;
an easy scramble onto his trousers,
pushing into the weave, trying to get a grip.
By the overhanging shirt I change
direction, traverse along his belt
to an earth-stained hand. The nails
are splintered and give good purchase,
the skin of his finger is smooth and thick
like warm ice. On his arm I discover
the glassy ridge of a scar, place my feet
gently in the old stitches and move on.
At his still firm shoulder, I rest for a while
in the shade, not looking down,
for climbing has its dangers, then pull
myself up the loose skin of his neck
to a smiling mouth to drink among teeth.
Refreshed, I cross the screed cheek,
to stare into his brown eyes, watch a pupil
slowly open and close. Then up over
the forehead, the wrinkles well-spaced
and easy, to his thick hair (soft and white
at this altitude), reaching for the summit,
where gasping for breath I can only lie
watching clouds and birds circle,
feeling his heat, knowing
the slow pulse of his good heart.

154   ANDREW WATERHOUSE

DUNBARTON

My Grandfather found
his grandchild's fogbound solitudes
sweeter than human society.

When Uncle Devereux died,
Daddy was still on sea-duty in the Pacific;
it seemed spontaneous and proper
for Mr. MacDonald, the farmer,
Karl, the chauffeur, and even my Grandmother
to say, "your Father." They meant my Grandfather.

He was my Father. I was his son.
On our yearly autumn get-aways from Boston
to the family graveyard in Dunbarton,
he took the wheel himself –
like an admiral at the helm.
Freed from Karl and chuckling over the gas
        he was saving,
he let his motor roller-coaster
out of control down each hill.
We stopped at the *Priscilla* in Nashua
for brownies and root-beer,
and later "pumped ship" together in the Indian
        Summer....

At the graveyard, a suave Venetian Christ
gave a sheepdog's nursing patience
to Grandfather's Aunt Lottie,
his Mother, the stone but not the bones
of his Father, Francis.
Failing as when Francis Winslow could count
them on his fingers,
the clump of virgin pine still stretched patchy
    ostrich necks
over the disused millpond's fragrantly woodstained
    water,
a reddish blur,
like the ever-blackening wine-dark coat
in our portrait of Edward Winslow
once sheriff for George the Second,
the sire of bankrupt Tories.

Grandfather and I
raked leaves from our dead forebears,
defied the dank weather
with "dragon" bonfires.

Our helper, Mr. Burroughs,
had stood with Sherman at Shiloh —
his thermos of shockless coffee
was milk and grounds;

his illegal home-made claret
was as sugary as grape jelly
in a tumbler capped with paraffin.

I borrowed Grandfather's cane
carved with the names and altitudes
of Norwegian mountains he had scaled –
more a weapon than a crutch.
I lanced it in the fauve ooze for newts.
In a tobacco tin after capture, the umber yellow
        mature newts
lost their leopard spots,
lay grounded as numb
as scrolls of candied grapefruit peel.
I saw myself as a young newt,
neurasthenic, scarlet
and wild in the wild coffee-colored water.

In the mornings I cuddled like a paramour
in my Grandfather's bed,
while he scouted about the chattering greenwood stove.

ELEGY FOR A GRANDFATHER

Flags breeze over tarmac in the club lot,
container ships steam up the coast,

smokestacks like cigars
between the loose lips of the bay.

Your nine iron drawn back for the swing,
a half-chuckle: that's where you left off,

in the surf of bees and grass
at the twelfth hole, the remnants

of the host beneath your tongue,
business card in pocket (President, American Shipping).

Curiosity was your business.
I ask you to come close.

Footsteps rustle in the witchgrass,
cotton cuffs switch past, the stalks stir.

How lucky it is I was born
to tell you the way it all turned out.

MY GRANDFATHER, DEAD LONG
BEFORE I WAS BORN

My grandfather, dead long before I was born,
died among strangers; and all the verse he wrote
was lost –
except for what
still speaks through me
as mine.

MAPLE SYRUP

August, goldenrod blowing. We walk
into the graveyard, to find
my grandfather's grave. Ten years ago
I came here last, bringing
marigolds from the round garden
outside the kitchen.
I didn't know you then.
                              We walk
among carved names that go with photographs
on top of the piano at the farm:
Keneston, Wells, Fowler, Batchelder, Buck.
We pause at the new grave
of Grace Fenton, my grandfather's
sister. Last summer
we called on her at the nursing home,
eighty-seven, and nodding
in a blue housedress. We cannot find
my grandfather's grave.
                              Back at the house
where no one lives, we potter
and explore the back chamber
where everything comes to rest: spinning wheels,
pretty boxes, quilts,
bottles, books, albums of postcards.
Then with a flashlight we descend

firm steps to the root cellar – black,
cobwebby, huge,
with dirt floors and fieldstone walls,
and above the walls, holding the hewn
sills of the house, enormous
granite foundation stones.
Past the empty bins
for squash, apples, carrots, and potatoes,
we discover the shelves for canning, a few
pale pints
of tomato left, and – what
is this? – syrup, maple syrup
in a quart jar, syrup
my grandfather made twenty-five
years ago
for the last time.
                    I remember
coming to the farm in March
in sugaring time, as a small boy.
He carried the pails of sap, sixteen-quart
buckets, dangling from each end
of a wooden yoke
that lay across his shoulders, and emptied them
into a vat in the saphouse

where fire burned day and night
for a week.
              Now the saphouse
tilts, nearly to the ground,
like someone exhausted
to the point of death, and next winter
when snow piles three feet thick
on the roofs of the cold farm,
the saphouse will shudder and slide
with the snow to the ground.
                      Today
we take my grandfather's last
quart of syrup
upstairs, holding it gingerly,
and we wash off twenty-five years
of dirt, and we pull
and pry the lid up, cutting the stiff,
dried rubber gasket, and dip our fingers
in, you and I both, and taste
the sweetness, you for the first time,
the sweetness preserved, of a dead man
in the kitchen he left
when his body slid
like anyone's into the ground.

SORROW, FURY,
REGRET

THE LITTLE BOY LOST

"Father, father, where are you going?
O do not walk so fast.
Speak, father, speak to your little boy
Or else I shall be lost."

The night was dark, no father was there,
The child was wet with dew.
The mire was deep, & the child did weep,
And away the vapor flew.

LORD ULLIN'S DAUGHTER

A chieftain, to the Highlands bound,
Cries, "Boatman, do not tarry!
And I'll give thee a silver pound
To row us o'er the ferry!" –

"Now, who be ye, would cross Lochgyle,
This dark and stormy weather?"
"O, I'm the chief of Ulva's isle,
And this, Lord Ullin's daughter. –

"And fast before her father's men
Three days we've fled together,
For should he find us in the glen,
My blood would stain the heather.

"His horsemen hard behind us ride;
Should they our steps discover,
Then who will cheer my bonny bride
When they have slain her lover?" –

Out spoke the hardy Highland wight, –
"I'll go, my chief – I'm ready: –
It is not for your silver bright;
But for your winsome lady:

"And by my word! the bonny bird
In danger shall not tarry;
So, though the waves are raging white,
I'll row you o'er the ferry." –

By this the storm grew loud apace,
The water-wraith was shrieking;
And in the scowl of heaven each face
Grew dark as they were speaking.

But still as wilder blew the wind,
And as the night grew drearer,
Adown the glen rode armèd men,
Their trampling sounded nearer. –

"O haste thee, haste!" the lady cries,
"Though tempests round us gather;
I'll meet the raging of the skies,
But not an angry father." –

The boat has left a stormy land,
A stormy sea before her, –
When, O! too strong for human hand,
The tempest gather'd o'er her.

And still they row'd amidst the roar
Of waters fast prevailing:
Lord Ullin reach'd that fatal shore, —
His wrath was changed to wailing.

For, sore dismay'd through storm and shade,
His child he did discover: —
One lovely hand she stretch'd for aid,
And one was round her lover.

"Come back! come back!" he cried in grief
"Across this stormy water:
And I'll forgive your Highland chief,
My daughter! — O my daughter!"

'Twas vain: the loud waves lash'd the shore,
Return or aid preventing:
The waters wild went o'er his child,
And he was left lamenting.

THE PORTRAIT

My mother never forgave my father
for killing himself,
especially at such an awkward time
and in a public park,
that spring
when I was waiting to be born.
She locked his name
in her deepest cabinet
and would not let him out,
though I could hear him thumping.
When I came down from the attic
with the pastel portrait in my hand
of a long-lipped stranger
with a brave moustache
and deep brown level eyes,
she ripped it into shreds
without a single word
and slapped me hard.
In my sixty-fourth year
I can feel my cheek
still burning.

RADIANT IVORY

After the death of my father, I locked
myself in my room, bored and animal-like.
The travel clock, the Johnnie Walker bottle,
the parrot tulips – everything possessed his face,
chaste and obscure. Snow and rain battered the air
white, insane, slathery. Nothing poured
out of me except sensibility, dilated.
It was as if I were *sub*-born – preverbal,
truculent, pure – with hard ivory arms
reaching out into a dark and crowded space,
illuminated like a perforated silver box
or a little room in which glowing cigarettes
came and went, like souls losing magnitude,
but none with the battered hand I knew.

TOURS

A girl on the stairs listens to her father
Beat up her mother.
Doors bang.
She comes down in her nightgown.

The piano stands there in the dark
Like a boy with an orchid.

She plays what she can
Then she turns the lamp on.

Her mother's music is spread out
On the floor like brochures.

She hears her father
Running through the leaves.

The last black key
She presses stays down, makes no sound
Someone putting their tongue where their tooth
        had been.

MY PAPA'S WALTZ

The whiskey on your breath
Could make a small boy dizzy;
But I hung on like death:
Such waltzing was not easy.

We romped until the pans
Slid from the kitchen shelf;
My mother's countenance
Could not undrown itself.

The hand that held my wrist
Was battered on one knuckle;
At every step you missed
My right ear scraped a buckle.

You beat time on my head
With a palm caked hard by dirt,
Then waltzed me off to bed
Still clinging to your shirt.

THE LESSON

"Your father's gone," my bald headmaster said.
His shiny dome and brown tobacco jar
Splintered at once in tears. It wasn't grief.
I cried for knowledge which was bitterer
Than any grief. For there and then I knew
That grief has uses – that a father dead
Could bind the bully's fist a week or two;
And then I cried for shame, then for relief.

I was a month past ten when I learnt this:
I still remember how the noise was stilled
In school-assembly when my grief came in.
Some goldfish in a bowl quietly sculled
Around their shining prison on its shelf.
They were indifferent. All the other eyes
Were turned towards me. Somewhere in myself
Pride, like a goldfish, flashed a sudden fin.

EDWARD LUCIE-SMITH   173

CIGARETTES

my father burned us all. ash
fell from his hand onto our beds,
onto our tables and chairs.
ours was the roof the sirens
rushed to at night
mistaking the glow of his pain
for flame. nothing is burning here,
my father would laugh, ignoring
my charred pillow, ignoring his own
smoldering halls.

OHIO

The horse staggers out of my sleep.
I follow him with my eye
down the blacktop past the football
field, his hooves clipping his knees,
I follow until I've climbed on his slippery back.
We ride like this for miles, nights.
Galloping past the rum hibiscus
and into the green moraines,
where we eat hard blue grass and
I begin to pray. O home!

My father never rode horses,
not even in his sleep, one hand curled on the arm chair,
the other propping up his head,
cushioning his ears. But he,
he was a horse from Troy,
a tinder, a tender, a ruse, a quack, a doctor.
A doctor! A man with a daughter upstairs
like a banked fire, a man with five daughters,
all like quiet fires, crackling and breathing,
until the four black horses
arrived at our buttoned windows,
with their brown eyes, and the curious noses
with which they sniff.

THE LOST PILOT
For My Father, 1922–1944

Your face did not rot
like the others – the co-pilot,
for example, I saw him

yesterday. His face is corn-
mush; his wife and daughter,
the poor ignorant people, stare

as if he will compose soon.
He was more wronged than Job.
But your face did not rot

like the others – it grew dark,
and hard like ebony;
the features progressed in their

distinction. If I could cajole
you to come back for an evening,
down from your compulsive

orbiting, I would touch you,
read your face as Dallas,
your hoodlum gunner, now,

with the blistered eyes, reads
his braille editions. I would
touch your face as a disinterested

scholar touches an original page.
However frightening, I would
discover you, and I would not

turn you in; I would not make
you face your wife, or Dallas,
or the co-pilot, Jim. You

could return to your crazy
orbiting, and I would not try
to fully understand what

it means to you. All I know
is this: when I see you,
as I have seen you at least

once every year of my life,
spin across the wilds of the sky
like a tiny, African god,

I feel dead. I feel as if I were
the residue of a stranger's life,
that I should pursue you.

My head cocked toward the sky,
I cannot get off the ground,
and, you, passing over again,

fast, perfect, and unwilling
to tell me that you are doing
well, or that it was mistake

that placed you in that world,
and me in this; or that misfortune
placed these worlds in us.

MY FATHER IN THE NIGHT
COMMANDING NO

My father in the night commanding No
Has work to do. Smoke issues from his lips;
    He reads in silence.
The frogs are croaking and the streetlamps glow.

And then my mother winds the gramophone;
The Bride of Lammermoor begins to shriek –
    Or reads a story
About a prince, a castle, and a dragon.

The moon is glimmering above the hill.
I stand before the gateposts of the King –
    So runs the story –
Of Thule, at midnight when the mice are still.

And I have been in Thule! It has come true –
The journey and the danger of the world,
    All that there is
To bear and to enjoy, endure and do.

Landscapes, seascapes ... where have I been led?
The names of cities – Paris, Venice, Rome –
    Held out their arms.
A feathered god, seductive, went ahead.

Here is my house. Under a red rose tree
A child is swinging; another gravely plays.
    They are not surprised
That I am here; they were expecting me.

And yet my father sits and reads in silence,
My mother sheds a tear, the moon is still,
    And the dark wind
Is murmuring that nothing ever happens.

Beyond his jurisdiction as I move
Do I not prove him wrong? And yet, it's true
    They will not change
There, on the stage of terror and of love.

The actors in that playhouse always sit
In fixed positions – father, mother, child
    With painted eyes.
How sad it is to be a little puppet!

Their heads are wooden. And you once pretended
To understand them! Shake them as you will,
    They cannot speak.
Do what you will, the comedy is ended.

Father, why did you work? Why did you weep,
Mother? Was the story so important?
    "Listen!" the wind
Said to the children, and they fell asleep.

DADDY

You do not do, you do not do
Any more, black shoe
In which I have lived like a foot
For thirty years, poor and white,
Barely daring to breathe or Achoo.

Daddy, I have had to kill you.
You died before I had time —
Marble-heavy, a bag full of God,
Ghastly statue with one grey toe
Big as a Frisco seal

And a head in the freakish Atlantic
Where it pours bean green over blue
In the waters off beautiful Nauset.
I used to pray to recover you.
Ach, du.

In the German tongue, in the Polish town
Scraped flat by the roller
Of wars, wars, wars.
But the name of the town is common.
My Polack friend

Says there are a dozen or two.
So I never could tell where you
Put your foot, your root,
I never could talk to you.
The tongue stuck in my jaw.

It stuck in a barb wire snare.
Ich, ich, ich, ich,
I could hardly speak.
I thought every German was you.
And the language obscene

An engine, an engine
Chuffing me off like a Jew.
A Jew to Dachau, Auschwitz, Belsen.
I began to talk like a Jew.
I think I may well be a Jew.

The snows of the Tyrol, the clear beer of Vienna
Are not very pure or true.
With my gypsy ancestress and my weird luck
And my Taroc pack and my Taroc pack
I may be a bit of a Jew.

I have always been scared of *you*,
With your Luftwaffe, your gobbledygoo.
And your neat moustache

And your Aryan eye, bright blue.
Panzer-man, panzer-man, O You —

Not God but a swastika
So black no sky could squeak through.
Every woman adores a Fascist,
The boot in the face, the brute
Brute heart of a brute like you.

You stand at the blackboard, daddy,
In the picture I have of you,
A cleft in your chin instead of your foot
But no less a devil for that, no not
Any less the black man who

Bit my pretty red heart in two.
I was ten when they buried you.
At twenty I tried to die
And get back, back, back to you.
I thought even the bones would do.

But they pulled me out of the sack,
And they stuck me together with glue.
And then I knew what to do.
I made a model of you,
A man in black with a Meinkampf look

And a love of the rack and the screw.
And I said I do, I do.
So daddy, I'm finally through.
The black telephone's off at the root,
The voices just can't worm through.

If I've killed one man, I've killed two —
The vampire who said he was you
And drank my blood for a year,
Seven years, if you want to know.
Daddy, you can lie back now.

There's a stake in your fat black heart
And the villagers never liked you.
They are dancing and stamping on you.
They always *knew* it was you.
Daddy, daddy, you bastard, I'm through.

AMERICAN PRIMITIVE

Look at him there in his stovepipe hat,
His high-top shoes, and his handsome collar;
Only my Daddy could look like that,
And I love my Daddy like he loves his Dollar.

The screen door bangs, and it sounds so funny
There he is in a shower of gold;
His pockets are stuffed with folding money,
His lips are blue, and his hands feel cold.

He hangs in the hall by his black cravat,
The ladies faint, and the children holler:
Only my Daddy could look like that,
And I love my Daddy like he loves his Dollar.

WILLIAM JAY SMITH

ELEGY FOR MY FATHER

Father, whom I murdered every night but one,
That one, when your death murdered me,
Your body waits within the wasting sod.
Clutching at the straw-face of your God,
Do you remember me, your morbid son,
Curled in a death, all motive unbegun,
Continuum of flesh, who never thought to be
The mourning mirror of your potency?

All you had battled for the nightmare took
Away, as dropping from your eyes, the sea-
Salt tears, with messages that none could read,
Impotent, pellucid, were the final seeds
You sowed. Above you, the white night nurse shook
His head, and, moaning on the moods of luck,
We knew the double-dealing enemy:
From pain you suffered, pain had set you free.

Down from the ceiling, father, circles came:
Angels, perhaps, to bear your soul away.
But tasting the persisting salt of pain,
I think my tears created them, though, in vain,
Like yours, they fell. All losses link: the same
Creature marred us both to stake his claim.
Shutting my eyelids, barring night and day,
I saw, and see, your body borne away.

Two months dead, I wrestle with your name
Whose separate letters make a paltry sum
That is not you. If still you harbor mine,
Think of the house we had in summertime
When in the sea-light every early game
Was played with love and, if death's waters came,
You'd rescue me. How I would take you from,
Now, if I could, its whirling vacuum.

ELEGIES: ILLNESS, LOSS, AND LETTING GO

ON MY FIRST SON

Farewell, thou child of my right hand, and joy;
My sin was too much hope of thee, loved boy.
Seven years thou wert lent to me, and I thee pay,
Exacted by thy fate, on the just day.
Oh, could I lose all father, now! For why
Will man lament the state he should envy?
To have so soon scaped world's and flesh's rage,
And, if no other misery, yet age!
Rest in soft peace, and, asked, say here doth lie
Ben Jonson his best piece of poetry;
For whose sake, henceforth, all his vows be such,
As what he loves may never like too much.

TO MY DEAR SON, GERVASE BEAUMONT

Can I, who have for others oft compiled
The songs of death, forget my sweetest child,
Which, like a flower crushed, with a blast is dead,
And ere full time hangs down his smiling head,
Expecting with clear hope to live anew,
Among the angels fed with heavenly dew?
We have this sign of joy, that many days,
While on the earth his struggling spirit stays,
The name of Jesus in his mouth contains,
His only food, his sleep, his ease from pains.
O may that sound be rooted in my mind,
Of which in him such strong effect I find.
Dear Lord, receive my son, whose winning love
To me was like a friendship, far above
The course of nature, or his tender age;
Whose looks could all my bitter griefs assuage;
Let his pure soul — ordained seven years to be
In that frail body, which was part of me —
Remain my pledge in heaven, as sent to show
How to this port at every step I go.

EPITAPH ON A CHILD

Here, freed from pain, secure from misery lies
A child, the darling of his parents' eyes:
A gentler lamb ne'er sported on the plain,
A fairer flower will never bloom again:
Few were the days allotted to his breath;
Now let him sleep in peace his night of death.

ON MY EVER HONOURED FATHER

O ye whose cheek the tear of pity stains,
Draw near with pious rev'rence, and attend!
Here lie the loving husband's dear remains,
The tender father, and the gen'rous friend;
The pitying heart that felt for human woe,
The dauntless heart that fear'd no human pride;
The friend of man – to vice alone a foe;
For "ev'n his failings lean'd to virtue's side."

METAMORPHOSIS

1 NIGHT
The angel of death flies
low over my father's bed.
Only my mother sees. She and my father
are alone in the room.

She bends over him to touch
his hand, his forehead. She is
so used to mothering
that now she strokes his body
as she would the other children's,
first gently, then
inured to suffering.

Nothing is any different.
Even the spot on the lung
was always there.

2 METAMORPHOSIS

My father has forgotten me
in the excitement of dying.
Like a child who will not eat,
he takes no notice of anything.

I sit at the edge of his bed
while the living circle us
like so many tree stumps.

Once, for the smallest
fraction of an instant, I thought
he was alive in the present again;
then he looked at me
as a blind man stares
straight into the sun, since
whatever it could do to him
is done already.

Then his flushed face
turned away from the contract.

3 FOR MY FATHER

I'm going to live without you
as I learned once
to live without my mother.
You think I don't remember that?
I've spent my whole life trying to remember.

Now, after so much solitude,
death doesn't frighten me,
not yours, not mine either.
And those words, *the last time*,
have no power over me. I know
intense love always leads to mourning.

For once, your body doesn't frighten me.
From time to time, I run my hand over your face
lightly, like a dustcloth.
What can shock me now? I feel
no coldness that can't be explained.
Against your cheek, my hand is warm
and full of tenderness.

NULLIPARA

The last morning of my visit, we sit
in our bathrobes, cronies, we cross and re-cross
our legs. Suddenly, he sees a thread
dangling from the cuff of my nightie, he cries out
Stay there! and goes to his desk drawer.
I hold my wrist out to him
and he stares with rigid concentration,
his irises balls of impacted matter.
He opens the shears, weighty and silvery-
brassy, the color of taint, he gets the
blades on either side of the thread
close to the cuff – he wants to get it
exactly right, to do me a service
at the end of his life. He snips once
and we sigh, we get fresh coffee and feel it
enter us. He knows he will live in me
after he is dead, I will carry him like a mother.
I do not know if I will ever deliver.

HIS TERROR

He loves the portable altar the minister
brings to the hospital, its tiny cruets and
phials, its cross that stands up
when the lid opens, like the ballerina who un-
bent, when I opened my jewelry box, she
rose and twirled like the dead. Then the lid
folded her down, bowing, in the dark,
the way I would wait, under my bed,
for morning. My father has forgotten that,
he opens his mouth for the porous disc
to be laid on his tongue, he loves to call the minister
    Father.
And yet, somewhere in his body, is there terror?
The lumps of the cancer are everywhere now,
he can lay his palm where they swell his skin, he can
finger the holes where the surgeon has been in him.
He asks me to touch them.
Maybe his terror is not of dying,
or even of death, but of some cry
he has kept inside him all his life
and there are weeks left.

HIS STILLNESS

The doctor said to my father, "You asked me
to tell you when nothing more could be done.
That's what I'm telling you now." My father
sat quite still, as he always did,
especially not moving his eyes. I had thought
he would rave if he understood he would die,
wave his arms and cry out. He sat up,
thin, and clean, in his clean gown,
like a holy man. The doctor said,
"There are things we can do which might give you time,
but we cannot cure you." My father said,
"Thank you." And he sat, motionless, alone,
with the dignity of a foreign leader.
I sat beside him. This was my father.
He had known he was mortal. I had feared they
        would have
to tie him down. I had not remembered
he had always held still and kept silent to bear things,
the liquor a way to keep still. I had not
known him. My father had dignity. At the
end of his life his life began
to wake in me.

EPITAPH UPON A CHILD
THAT DIED

Here she lies, a pretty bud,
Lately made of flesh and blood:
Who as soon fell fast asleep
As her little eyes did peep.
Give her strewings, but not stir
The earth that lightly covers her.

THE CHILDLESS FATHER

"Up, Timothy, up with your staff and away!
Not a soul in the village this morning will stay;
The hare has just started from Hamilton's grounds,
And Skiddaw is glad with the cry of the hounds."

— Of coats and of jackets grey, scarlet, and green,
On the slopes of the pastures all colours were seen;
With their comely blue aprons, and caps white as snow,
The girls on the hills made a holiday show.

Fresh sprigs of green box-wood, not six months before,
Filled the funeral basin at Timothy's door;
A coffin through Timothy's threshold had past;
One Child did it bear, and that Child was his last.

Now fast up the dell came the noise and the fray,
The horse and the horn, and the hark! hark away!
Old Timothy took up his staff, and he shut
With a leisurely motion the door of his hut.

Perhaps to himself at that moment he said;
"The key I must take, for my Ellen is dead."
But of this in my ears not a word did he speak;
And he went to the chase with a tear on his cheek.

GOD GAVE TO ME A CHILD IN PART

God gave to me a child in part,
Yet wholly gave the father's heart:
Child of my soul, O whither now,
Unborn, unmothered, goest thou?

You came, you went, and no man wist;
Hapless, my child, no breast you kist;
On no dear knees, a privileged babbler, clomb,
Nor knew the kindly feel of home.

My voice may reach you, O my dear –
A father's voice perhaps the child may hear;
And, pitying, you may turn your view
On that poor father whom you never knew.

Alas! alone he sits, who then,
Immortal among mortal men,
Sat hand in hand with love, and all day through
With your dear mother wondered over you.

ROBERT LOUIS STEVENSON 203

THE ERL-KING

Who rides there so late through the night dark
    and drear?
The father it is, with his infant so dear;
He holdeth the boy tightly clasp'd in his arm,
He holdeth him safely, he keepeth him warm.

"My son, wherefore seek'st thou thy face thus to hide?"
"Look, father, the Erl-King is close by our side!
Dost see not the Erl-King, with crown and with train?"
"My son, 'tis the mist rising over the plain."

"Oh, come, thou dear infant! oh come thou with me!
Full many a game I will play there with thee;
On my strand, lovely flowers their blossoms unfold,
My mother shall grace thee with garments of gold."

"My father, my father, and dost thou not hear
The words that the Erl-King now breathes in mine ear?"
"Be calm, dearest child, 'tis thy fancy deceives;
'Tis the sad wind that sighs through the withering
    leaves."

"Wilt go, then, dear infant, wilt go with me there?
My daughters shall tend thee with sisterly care
My daughters by night their glad festival keep,
They'll dance thee, and rock thee, and sing thee
        to sleep."

"My father, my father, and dost thou not see,
How the Erl-King his daughters has brought here
        for me?"
"My darling, my darling, I see it aright,
'Tis the aged grey willows deceiving thy sight."

"I love thee, I'm charm'd by thy beauty, dear boy!
And if thou'rt unwilling, then force I'll employ."
"My father, my father, he seizes me fast,
Full sorely the Erl-King has hurt me at last."

The father now gallops, with terror half wild,
He grasps in his arms the poor shuddering child;
He reaches his courtyard with toil and with dread, –
The child in his arms finds he motionless, dead.

PARKINSON'S DISEASE

While spoon-feeding him with one hand
she holds his hand with her other hand,
or rather lets it rest on top of his,
which is permanently clenched shut.
When he turns his head away, she reaches
around and puts in the spoonful blind.
He will not accept the next morsel
until he has completely chewed this one.
His bright squint tells her he finds
the shrimp she has just put in delicious.
She strokes his head very slowly, as if
to cheer up each hair sticking up
from its root in his stricken brain.
Standing behind him, she presses
her cheek to his, kisses his jowl,
and his eyes seem to stop seeing
and do nothing but emit light.
Could heaven be a time, after we are dead,
of remembering the knowledge
flesh had from flesh? The flesh
of his face is hard, perhaps
from years spent facing down others
until they fell back, and harder
from years of being himself faced down
and falling back, and harder still
from all the while frowning

and beaming and worrying and shouting
and probably letting go in rages.
His face softens into a kind
of quizzical wince, as if one
of the other animals were working at
getting the knack of the human smile.
When picking up a cookie he uses
both thumbtips to grip it
and push it against an index finger
to secure it so that he can lift it.
She takes him to the bathroom,
and when they come out, she is facing him,
walking backwards in front of him
holding his hands, pulling him
when he stops, reminding him to step
when he forgets and starts to pitch forward.
She is leading her old father into the future
as far as they can go, and she is walking
him back into her childhood, where she stood
in bare feet on the toes of his shoes
and they foxtrotted on this same rug.
I watch them closely: she could be teaching him
the last steps that one day she may teach me.
At this moment, he glints and shines,
as if it will be only a small dislocation
for him to pass from this paradise into the next.

GALWAY KINNELL

THE STRAIT-JACKETS

I lay the suitcase on Father's bed
and unzip it slowly, gently.
Inside, packed in cloth strait-jackets
lie forty live hummingbirds
tied down in rows, each tiny head
cushioned on a swaddled body.
I feed them from a flask of sugar water,
inserting every bill into the pipette,
then unwind their bindings
so Father can see their changing colours
as they dart around his room.
They hover inches from his face
as if he's a flower, their humming
just audible above the oxygen recycler.
For the first time since I've arrived
he's breathing easily, the cannula
attached to his nostrils almost slips out.
I don't know how long we sit there
but when I next glance at his face
he's asleep, lights from their feathers
still playing on his eyelids and cheeks.
It takes me hours to catch them all
and wrap them in their strait-jackets.
I work quietly, he's in such
a deep sleep he doesn't wake once.

BENEVOLENCE

When my father dies and comes back as a dog,
I already know what his favorite sound will be:
the soft, almost inaudible gasp
as the rubber lips of the refrigerator door
unstick, followed by that arctic

exhalation of cold air;
then the cracking of the ice-cube tray above the sink
and the quiet *ching* the cubes make
when dropped into a glass.

Unable to pronounce the name of his favorite drink,
        or to express
his preference for single malt,
he will utter one sharp bark
and point the wet black arrow of his nose
imperatively up
at the bottle on the shelf,

then seat himself before me,
trembling, expectant, water pouring
down the long pink dangle of his tongue
as the memory of pleasure from his former life
shakes him like a tail.

What I'll remember as I tower over him,
holding a dripping, whiskey-flavored cube
above his open mouth,
relishing the power rushing through my veins
the way it rushed through his,

what I'll remember as I stand there
is the hundred clever tricks
I taught myself to please him,
and for how long I mistakenly believed
that it was love he held concealed in his closed hand.

MY FATHER IS SHRINKING

When we last hugged each other
in the garage,
our two heads were level.
Over his shoulder I could see
potato-sacks.

Another season
and in the dusty sunlight
I shall gather him to me,
smooth his collar,
bend to listen
for his precious breathing.

When he reaches
to my waist,
I shall no longer
detach his small hands
from my skirt,
escape his shrill voice
in the dawn garden.

When he comes to my knees,
I shall pick him up and rock him,
rub my face on the white
stubble of his cheek,

see his silver skull
gleam up at me
through thin combings.

POEM FOR MY FATHER'S GHOST

Now is my father
A traveler, like all the bold men
He talked of, endlessly
And with boundless admiration,
Over the supper table,
Or gazing up from his white pillow –
Book on his lap always, until
Even that grew too heavy to hold.

Now is my father free of all binding fevers.
Now is my father
Traveling where there is no road.

Finally, he could not lift a hand
To cover his eyes.
Now he climbs to the eye of the river,
He strides through the Dakotas,
He disappears into the mountains. And though he looks
Cold and hungry as any man
At the end of a questing season,

He is one of *them* now:
He cannot be stopped.

Now is my father
Walking the wind,
Sniffing the deep Pacific
That begins at the end of the world.

Vanished from us utterly,
Now is my father circling the deepest forest –
Then turning in to the last red campfire burning
In the final hills,

Where chieftains, warriors and heroes
Rise and make him welcome,
Recognizing, under the shambles of his body,
A brother who has walked his thousand miles.

THRESHOLD

My father is dying. I cannot breathe.
He is leaving home, and I now must try
to close the door and lock it with his key.

He no longer inhabits the moth-wing
pages from the book of childhood, but travels
beyond the door, inside the past, concealed

behind the rack of clothes, the story's attic,
the place he would describe before I fell asleep.
The book lies open on the pillow.

I shut my eyes, try to count stars or stairs climbing
always beyond reach. It's too soon for him to leave.
I still must learn to place

one foot before the other and to wake
the words from sleeping letters, so I wait
for him to read the book. When day turns dark,

the key revolves, and he, with bear-tight arms,
catches me all in air – I ride his shoe
across the wood to the unending hall.

TERMINAL DAYS AT BEVERLY FARMS

At Beverly Farms, a portly, uncomfortable boulder
bulked in the garden's center —
an irregular Japanese touch.
After his Bourbon "old fashioned," Father,
bronzed, breezy, a shade too ruddy,
swayed as if on deck duty
under his six pointed star-lantern —
last July's birthday present.
He smiled his oval Lowell smile,
he wore his cream gabardine dinner-jacket,
and indigo cummerbund.
His head was efficient and hairless,
his newly dieted figure was vitally trim.

Father and Mother moved to Beverly Farms
to be a two-minute walk from the station,
half an hour by train from the Boston doctors.
They had no sea-view,
but sky-blue tracks of the commuters' railroad shone
like a double-barreled shotgun
through the scarlet late August sumac,
multiplying like cancer
at their garden's border.

Father had had two coronaries.
He still treasured underhand economies,
but his best friend was his little black Chevy,
garaged like a sacrificial steer
with gilded hooves,
yet sensationally sober,
and with less side than an old dancing pump.
The local dealer, a "buccaneer,"
had been bribed a "king's ransom"
to quickly deliver a car without chrome.

Each morning at eight-thirty,
inattentive and beaming,
loaded with his "calc" and "trig" books,
his clipper ship statistics,
and his ivory slide rule,
Father stole off with the Chevy
to loaf in the Maritime Museum at Salem.
He called the curator
"the commander of the Swiss Navy."

Father's death was abrupt and unprotesting.
His vision was still twenty-twenty.
After a morning of anxious, repetitive smiling,
his last words to Mother were:
"I feel awful."

ROBERT LOWELL   217

WALK, NIGHT FALLING, MEMORY
OF MY FATHER

Downhill into town
between the flaring azaleas
of neighbor gardens: a cairn of fresh-
cut logs gives off a glow of
broken but transfigured flesh.

My father meeting me years ago
off a train at Kingsbridge: greenish
tweed cap, tan gabardine, leaning
on a rolled umbrella, the sun
in his eyes, the brown planes of his face
in shadow, and all of a sudden
old. The distance between us
closing to an awkward
stumbling embrace. Little left

but bits and pieces: pints in Healy's
before tea; a drive with visitors
to Sally Gap; my daughter making
game with his glasses; the transatlantic calls
for an anniversary, a birthday,
or to the hospital
before his operations. Moments
during those last days

in the ward, under the big window
where the clouds over the golf course
would break or darken, his unexpected
rise to high spirits, my hand
helping his hand
hold the glass of water. And one memory
he kept coming back to: being
a child in a white frock
watching his mother and another woman
in long white dresses and broad straw hats
recline in a rowing boat on the Boyne
near Navan: how the boat rocked
side to side, the women smiling and
talking in low voices, and him sitting
by himself in a pool of sunshine
on the bank, his little feet barely
reaching the cool water. I remember
how the nurses swaddled his
thin legs in elastic bandages, keeping him
together for a day or two. By the time

I'm walking uphill again, the dark
is down and the night voices are
at their prayers and panicky conjurations:

one thrush shapes the air around him
like someone revising the day's
wild outpour to a few lines; fireflies
wink on and off in lovers' Morse, my own
head floating among them, seeing
as each opens its heart in silence
and in silence closes
just how large the dark is. White moths

brush by on ghostly wings; new moonlight
casts across this shaking summer world
a thin, translucent skin of snow. Indoors
I watch the moths – fallen angels the size
and shade of Communion wafers –
beat dusted wings against the screen,
flinging themselves
at this impossible light.

WHITE APPLES

when my father had been dead a week
I woke
with his voice in my ear
                              I sat up in bed
and held my breath
and stared at the pale closed door

white apples and the taste of stone

if he called again
I would put on my coat and galoshes

I SEE YOU DANCING, FATHER

No sooner downstairs after the night's rest
And in the door
Than you started to dance a step
In the middle of the kitchen floor.

And as you danced
You whistled.
You made your own music
Always in tune with yourself.

Well, nearly always, anyway.
You're buried now
In Lislaughtin Abbey
And whenever I think of you

I go back beyond the old man
Mind and body broken
To find the unbroken man.
It is the moment before the dance begins,

Your lips are enjoying themselves
Whistling an air.
Whatever happens or cannot happen
In the time I have to spare
I see you dancing, father.

DO NOT GO GENTLE INTO
THAT GOOD NIGHT

Do not go gentle into that good night,
Old age should burn and rave at close of day;
Rage, rage against the dying of the light.

Though wise men at their end know dark is right,
Because their words had forked no lightning they
Do not go gentle into that good night.

Good men, the last wave by, crying how bright
Their frail deeds might have danced in a green bay,
Rage, rage against the dying of the light.

Wild men who caught and sang the sun in flight,
And learn, too late, they grieved it on its way,
Do not go gentle into that good night.

Grave men, near death, who see with blinding sight
Blind eyes could blaze like meteors and be gay,
Rage, rage against the dying of the light.

And you, my father, there on the sad height,
Curse, bless me now with your fierce tears, I pray.
Do not go gentle into that good night.
Rage, rage against the dying of the light.

DYLAN THOMAS   223

THE DRUNKARD'S CHILD

He stood beside his dying child,
With a dim and bloodshot eye;
They'd won him from the haunts of vice
To see his first-born die.
He came with a slow and staggering tread,
A vague, unmeaning stare,
And, reeling, clasped the clammy hand,
So deathly pale and fair.

In a dark and gloomy chamber,
Life ebbing fast away,
On a coarse and wretched pallet,
The dying sufferer lay:
A smile of recognition
Lit up the glazing eye;
"I'm very glad," it seemed to say,
"You've come to see me die."

That smile reached to his callous heart,
It sealed fountains stirred;
He tried to speak, but on his lips
Faltered and died each word.
And burning tears like rain
Poured down his bloated face,
Where guilt, remorse and shame
Had scathed, and left their trace.

"My father!" said the dying child,
(His voice was faint and low,)
"Oh! clasp me closely to your heart,
And kiss me ere I go.
Bright angels beckon me away,
To the holy city fair –
Oh! tell me, Father, ere I go,
Say, will you meet me there?"

He clasped him to his throbbing heart,
"I will! I will!" he said;
His pleading ceased – the father held
His first-born and his dead!
The marble brow, with golden curls,
Lay lifeless on his breast;
Like sunbeams on the distant clouds
Which line the gorgeous west.

FRANCES ELLEN WATKINS

STRAWBERRIES

When my father died I saw   a narrow valley

it looked as though it began   across the river
from the landing where he was born   but there was
                                                no river

I was hoeing the sand   of a small vegetable plot
for my mother   in deepening twilight
and looked up in time   to see a farm wagon
dry and gray   horse already hidden
and no driver   going into the valley
carrying a casket

                and another wagon
coming out of the valley   behind a gray horse
with a boy driving   and a high load
of two kinds of berries   one of them strawberries

        that night when I slept   I dreamed of things
wrong in the house   all of them signs
the water of the shower   running brackish
and an insect of a kind   I had seen him kill
climbing around   the walls of his bathroom
        up in the morning   I stopped on the stairs
my mother was awake   already and asked me
if I wanted a shower   before breakfast
and for breakfast she said   we have strawberries

From DREAM SONGS
(no. 384)

The marker slants, flowerless, day's almost done,
I stand above my father's grave with rage,
often, often before
I've made this awful pilgrimage to one
who cannot visit me, who tore his page
out: I come back for more,

I spit upon this dreadful banker's grave
who shot his heart out in a Florida dawn
O ho alas alas
When will indifference come, I moan & rave
I'd like to scrabble till I got right down
away down under the grass

and ax the casket open ha to see
just how he's taking it, which he sought so hard
we'll tear apart
the mouldering grave clothes ha & then Henry
will heft the ax once more, his final card,
and fell it on the start.

VISION IN BLACK AND WHITE

leaning back in a Naugahyde
covered recliner
reading proofs

I flash on my father stepping carefully
in hightop shoes
in nineteen hundred and twelve

across a road
all wagon tracks and mud
alive in the sun

to someone waiting on the other side
I think a woman

I give my attention to him
and the image breaks
I go back to my proofs
and he starts across again

The problem is not to notice
The problem is to let him go

SEEING THE SICK

Anointed and all, my father did remind me
Of Hopkins's Felix Randal.
                    And then he grew
(As he would have said himself) "wee in his clothes" –
Spectral, a relict –
                 And seemed to have grown so
Because of something spectral he'd thrown off,
The unbelonging, moorland part of him
That was Northumbrian, the bounden he
Who had walked the streets of Hexham at eighteen
With his stick and task of bringing home the dead
Body of his uncle by cattle-ferry.

Ghost-drover from the start. Brandisher of keel.

None of your fettled and bright battering sandal.

Cowdung coloured tweed and ox-blood leather.

The assessor's eye, the tally-keeper's head
For what beasts were on what land in what year . . .
But then that went as well. And all precaution.
His smile a summer half-door opening out
And opening in. A reprieving light.
For which the tendered morphine had our thanks.

SEAMUS HEANEY

ELEGY FOR MY FATHER
(Robert Strand 1908–68)

1 THE EMPTY BODY

The hands were yours, the arms were yours,
But you were not there.
The eyes were yours, but they were closed and
        would not open.
The distant sun was there.
The moon poised on the hill's white shoulder was there.
The wind on Bedford Basin was there.
The pale green light of winter was there.
Your mouth was there,
But you were not there.
When somebody spoke, there was no answer.
Clouds in the blind air came down
And buried the buildings along the water,
And the water was silent.
The gulls stared.
The years, the hours, that would not find you
Turned in the wrists of others.
There was no pain. It had gone.
There were no secrets. There was nothing to say.
The shade scattered its ashes.
The body was yours, but you were not there.
The air shivered against its skin.
The dark leaned into its eyes.
But you were not there.

2 ANSWERS

Why did you travel?

Because the house was cold.

Why did you travel?

Because it is what I have always done between sunset
and sunrise.

What did you wear?

I wore a blue suit, a white shirt, yellow tie, and yellow socks.

What did you wear?

I wore nothing. A scarf of pain kept me warm.

Who did you sleep with?

I slept with a different woman each night.

Who did you sleep with?

I slept alone. I have always slept alone.

Why did you lie to me?

I always thought I told the truth.

Why did you lie to me?

Because the truth lies like nothing else and I love the truth.

Why are you going?

Because nothing means much to me anymore.

Why are you going?

I don't know. I have never known.

How long shall I wait for you?

Do not wait for me. I am tired and I want to lie down.

Are you tired and do you want to lie down?

Yes, I am tired and I want to lie down.

3 YOUR DYING

Nothing could stop you.
Not the best day. Not the quiet. Not the ocean
  rocking.
You went on with your dying.
Not the trees
Under which you walked, not the trees that shaded
  you.
Not the doctor
Who warned you, the white-haired young doctor
  who saved you once.
You went on with your dying.
Nothing could stop you. Not your son. Not your
  daughter
Who fed you and made you into a child again.
Not your son who thought you would live forever.
Not the wind that shook your lapels.
Not the stillness that offered itself to your motion.
Not your shoes that grew heavier.
Not your eyes that refused to look ahead.
Nothing could stop you.
You sat in your room and stared at the city
And went on with your dying.
You went to work and let the cold enter your clothes.
You let blood seep into your socks.
Your face turned white.
Your voice cracked in two.

You leaned on your cane.
But nothing could stop you.
Not your friends who gave you advice.
Not your son. Not your daughter who watched you
    grow small.
Not fatigue that lived in your sighs.
Not your lungs that would fill with water.
Not your sleeves that carried the pain of your arms.
Nothing could stop you.
You went on with your dying.
When you played with children you went on
    with your dying.
When you sat down to eat,
When you woke up at night, wet with tears,
    your body sobbing,
You went on with your dying.
Nothing could stop you.
Not the past.
Not the future with its good weather.
Not the view from your window, the view of
    the graveyard.
Not the city. Not the terrible city with its wooden
    buildings.
Not defeat. Not success.
You did nothing but go on with your dying.
You put your watch to your ear.
You felt yourself slipping.

You lay on the bed.
You folded your arms over your chest and you
dreamed of the world without you,
Of the space under the trees,
Of the space in your room,
Of the spaces that would now be empty of you,
And you went on with your dying.
Nothing could stop you.
Not your breathing. Not your life.
Not the life you wanted.
Not the life you had.
Nothing could stop you.

4 YOUR SHADOW

You have your shadow.
The places where you were have given it back.
The hallways and bare lawns of the orphanage have
    given it back.
The Newsboys Home has given it back.
The streets of New York have given it back and so
    have the streets of Montreal.
The rooms in Belém where lizards would snap at
    mosquitos have given it back.
The dark streets of Manaus and the damp streets
    of Rio have given it back.
Mexico City where you wanted to leave it has given
    it back.
And Halifax where the harbor would wash its hands
    of you has given it back.
You have your shadow.
When you traveled the white wake of your going sent
    your shadow below, but when you arrived it was
    there to greet you. You had your shadow.
The doorways you entered lifted your shadow from
    you and when you went out, gave it back.
    You had your shadow.
Even when you forgot your shadow, you found it
    again; it had been with you.
Once in the country the shade of a tree covered your
    shadow and you were not known.

235

Once in the country you thought your shadow had
been cast by somebody else. Your shadow said
nothing.
Your clothes carried your shadow inside; when you
took them off, it spread like the dark of your past.
And your words that float like leaves in an air that
is lost, in a place no one knows, gave you back
your shadow.
Your friends gave you back your shadow.
Your enemies gave you back your shadow. They said
it was heavy and would cover your grave.
Your wife took your shadow and said she would keep it;
she died and you found it beside you on the bed.
You hated the sun because in the morning it would
take your shadow and at night would give it back
unused, untouched.
The night was good because it was your shadow and
you were large surrounding the moon.
Winter took your shadow which lay like a long cape
on the snow and gave it back with your breath.
When you died your shadow slept at the mouth of
the furnace and ate ashes for bread.
It rejoiced among ruins.
It watched while others slept.
It shone like crystal among the tombs.
It composed itself like air.
It wanted to be like snow on water.

It wanted to be nothing, but that was not possible.
It came to my house.
It sat on my shoulders.
Your shadow is yours. I told it so. I said it was yours.
I have carried it with me too long. I give it back.

5 MOURNING

They mourn for you.
When you rise at midnight,
And the dew glitters on the stone of your cheeks,
They mourn for you.
They lead you back into the empty house.
They carry the chairs and tables inside.
They sit you down and teach you to breathe.
And your breath burns,
It burns the pine box and the ashes fall like sunlight.
They give you a book and tell you to read.
They listen and their eyes fill with tears.
The women stroke your fingers.
They comb the yellow back into your hair.
They shave the frost from your beard.
They knead your thighs.
They dress you in fine clothes.
They rub your hands to keep them warm.
They feed you. They offer you money.
They get on their knees and beg you not to die.
When you rise at midnight they mourn for you.
They close their eyes and whisper your name
        over and over.
But they cannot drag the buried light from your veins.
They cannot reach your dreams.
Old man, there is no way.
Rise and keep rising, it does no good.
They mourn for you the way they can.

6 THE NEW YEAR

It is winter and the new year.
Nobody knows you.
Away from the stars, from the rain of light,
You lie under the weather of stones.
There is no thread to lead you back.
Your friends doze in the dark
Of pleasure and cannot remember.
Nobody knows you. You are the neighbor of nothing.
You do not see the rain falling and the man walking
       away,
The soiled wind blowing its ashes across the city.
You do not see the sun dragging the moon like
       an echo.
You do not see the bruised heart go up in flames,
The skulls of the innocent turn into smoke.
You do not see the scars of plenty, the eyes
       without light.
It is over. It is winter and the new year.
The meek are hauling their skins into heaven.
The hopeless are suffering the cold with those
       who have nothing to hide.
It is over and nobody knows you.
There is starlight drifting on the black water.
There are stones in the sea no one has seen.
There is a shore and people are waiting.
And nothing comes back.

239

Because it is over.
Because there is silence instead of a name.
Because it is winter and the new year.

INDEX OF AUTHORS

THOMAS BAILEY ALDRICH (1836–1907):
  Alec Yeaton's Son   77
YEHUDA AMICHAI (1924–2000):
  My Son, My Son, My Head, My Head   114
THOMAS BASTARD (1566–1618):
  De Puero Balbutiente   81
JOHN BEAUMONT (1583–1627):
  To My Dear Son, Gervase Beaumont   192
JOHN BERRYMAN (1914–72):
  From Dream Songs   107
  From Dream Songs   227
ELIZABETH BISHOP (1911–79): For Grandfather   151
SOPHIE CABOT BLACK (1958–): To Her Father . .   55
  Turning Away   61
  Brunnhilde, to Her Father   71
WILLIAM BLAKE (1757–1827): Infant Joy   24
  Infant Sorrow   25
  A Cradle Song   31
  The Little Boy Lost.   165
ANNE BRADSTREET (*c.* 1612–72):
  To Her Father with Some Verses   50
JOSEPH BRODSKY (1940–96):
  Odysseus to Telemachus   115
ELIZABETH BARRETT BROWNING (1806–61):
  To My Father on His Birthday   65

ROBERT BURNS (1759–96): A Poet's Welcome to
His Love-begotten Daughter 134
On My Ever Honoured Father 194
THOMAS CAMPBELL (1777–1844):
Lord Ullin's Daughter 166
WILLIAM CANTON (1845–1926): Laus Infantium 38
RAYMOND CARVER (1938–88): Photograph of
My Father in His Twenty-second Year . . 122
LUCILLE CLIFTON (1936–): cigarettes 174
HENRI COLE (1956–): Radiant Ivory 170
SAMUEL TAYLOR COLERIDGE (1772–1834):
Sonnet: On Receiving a Letter Informing
Me of the Birth of a Son 33
From Frost at Midnight 34
To an Infant 36
THOMAS DEKKER (*c.* 1570–*c.* 1632):
"Golden slumbers kiss your eyes" 19
RUSSELL EDSON (1935–): The Changeling . . . 120
EUGENE FIELD (1850–95):
Inscription for My Little Son's Silver Plate 109
DEBORAH GARRISON (1965–):
Dad, You Returned to Me This Morning . . 67
LOUISE GLÜCK (1943–): Snow 60
Telemachus' Fantasy 117
Metamorphosis 195
JOHANN WOLFGANG VON GOETHE (1749–1832):
The Erl-King 204

THOMAS GRAY (1716–71): Epitaph on a Child .. 193

DEBORA GREGER (1949–):

    The Armorer's Daughter 57

EAMON GRENNAN (1941–):

    Walk, Night Falling, Memory of My Father 218

DONALD HALL (1928–):

    My Son My Executioner 43

    Maple Syrup 160

    White Apples 221

GWEN HARWOOD (1920–95): For My Father .. 59

SEAMUS HEANEY (1939–): Follower 98

    Digging 100

    The Nod 102

    Seeing the Sick 229

ROBERT HERRICK (1591–1674):

    Epitaph upon a Child that Died 210

TONY HOAGLAND (1953–): Benevolence 209

HOMER (c. 750 B.C.): From The Iliad, Book VI .. 75

THOMAS HOOD (1799–1845):

    A Parental Ode to My Son, Aged Three

    Years and Five Months 92

GERARD MANLEY HOPKINS (1844–89):

    The Child Is Father to the Man 95

ANDREW HUDGINS (1951–):

    Elegy for My Father, Who Is Not Dead .. 110

TED HUGHES (1930–98): Dust as We Are 96

    Full Moon and Little Frieda 141

MURRAY JACKSON (1926–2002): Gifts 124

BEN JONSON (1572–1637):

    On My First Daughter 133

    On My First Son 191

BRENDAN KENNELLY (1936–):

    I See You Dancing, Father 222

CHARLES KINGSLEY (1819–75): To a Child 132

GALWAY KINNELL (1927–):

    The Olive Wood Fire 42

    After Making Love We Hear Footsteps . . 103

    Parkinson's Disease 206

RUDYARD KIPLING (1865–1936): Seal Lullaby . . 37

STANLEY KUNITZ (1905–2006): The Portrait . . 169

SIDNEY LANIER (1842–81): Baby Charley 29

D. H. LAWRENCE (1885–1930):

    A Baby Asleep After Pain 30

MICHAEL LONGLEY (1939–): The Branch 111

ROBERT LOWELL (1917–77): Dunbarton 155

    Terminal Days at Beverly Farms 216

EDWARD LUCIE-SMITH (1933–): The Lesson . . 173

GEORGE MACDONALD (1824–1905): The Baby . . 27

W. S. MERWIN (1927–):

    Grandfather in the Old Men's Home 152

    Strawberries 226

CZESLAW MILOSZ (1911–2004):

    Father in the Library 112

    Father's Incantations 113

HOWARD MOSS (1922–87):
    Elegy for My Father 186
HARRYETTE MULLEN (1953–):
    Father (Part 1) 66
RICHARD MURPHY (1927–): Natural Son 40
HOWARD NEMEROV (1920–91):
    September, the First Day of School 105
NAOMI SHIHAB NYE (1952–):
    My Father and the Figtree 53
SHARON OLDS (1942–): Nullipara 198
    His Terror 199
    His Stillness 200
MARY OLIVER (1935–):
    Poem for My Father's Ghost 214
GEORGE OPPEN (1908–84):
    Sara in Her Father's Arms 140
MEGHAN O'ROURKE (1976–):
    Elegy for a Grandfather 158
    Ohio 175
ELISE PASCHEN (1959–): Threshold 215
BORIS PASTERNAK (1890–1960): Hamlet 119
COVENTRY PATMORE (1823–96): The Toys . . . 90
PASCALE PETIT (1953–): The Strait-jackets 208
SYLVIA PLATH (1932–63): Daddy 181
KATHA POLLITT (1949–): A Chinese Bowl 62
KENNETH REXROTH (1905–82):
    The American Century 39

CHARLES REZNIKOFF (1894–1976): My
    Grandfather, Dead Long Before I Was Born   159
THEODORE ROETHKE (1908–63):
    My Papa's Waltz 172
GJERTRUD SCHNACKENBERG (1953–):
    Supernatural Love 47
SIR WALTER SCOTT (1771–1832):
    Lullaby of an Infant Chief 41
WILLIAM SHAKESPEARE (1564–1616):
    From Henry IV, Part 2 76
    From King Lear 131
PERCY BYSSHE SHELLEY (1792–1822):
    To William Shelley 82
    To Ianthe 136
JASON SHINDER (1955–): The Past 123
LOUIS SIMPSON (1923–):
    My Father in the Night Commanding No . . 179
WILLIAM J. SMITH (1918–): American Primitive 185
STEPHEN SPENDER (1909–95): To My Daughter 139
WILLIAM STAFFORD (1914–93): Listening 108
FRANK L. STANTON (1857–1927):
    Mighty Like a Rose 80
ROBERT LOUIS STEVENSON (1850–94):
    God Gave to Me a Child in Part 203
MARK STRAND (1934–):
    For Jessica, My Daughter 137
    Elegy for My Father 230

SU TUNG-P'O (1037–1101):
    On the Birth of His Son 26
ALGERNON CHARLES SWINBURNE (1837–1909):
    Étude Réaliste 20
    "Child, when they say that others" 85
JAMES TATE (1943–): The Lost Pilot 176
SARA TEASDALE (1884–1933):
    Grandfather's Love 153
ALFRED, LORD TENNYSON (1809–92):
    "Sweet and low, sweet and low" 22
DYLAN THOMAS (1914–53):
    Do Not Go Gentle into That Good Night . . 223
NATASHA TRETHEWEY (1966–):
    Amateur Fighter 69
ANDREW WATERHOUSE (1958–2001):
    Climbing My Grandfather 154
FRANCES ELLEN WATKINS (1825–1911):
    The Drunkard's Child 224
SUSAN WICKS (1947–): My Father Is Shrinking . . 211
RICHARD WILBUR (1921–):
    My Father Paints the Summer 126
    The Writer 142
MILLER WILLIAMS (1930–):
    Vision in Black and White 228
WILLIAM WORDSWORTH (1770–1850):
    Anecdote for Fathers 87
    The Childless Father 202

HENRY CLAY WORK (1832–84):
    Come Home, Father!   51
C. D. WRIGHT (1949–): Tours   171
W. B. YEATS (1865–1939): A Cradle Song   23
    A Prayer for My Daughter 144

ACKNOWLEDGMENTS

Thanks are due to the following copyright holders for permission to reprint:

YEHUDA AMICHAI: "My Son, My Son, My Head, My Head" from *Yehuda Amichai: A Life of Poetry 1948–1994* by Yehuda Amichai. Translated by Benjamin and Barbara Harshav, copyright © 1994 by HarperCollins Publishers, Inc. Hebrew-language version copyright © 1994 by Yehuda Amichai. Reprinted by permission of HarperCollins Publishers. JOHN BERRYMAN: Dream Song 241 "Father being the loneliest word" and Dream Song 384 "The marker slants" from *The Dream Songs* by John Berryman. Copyright © 1969 by John Berryman. Copyright renewed 1997 by Kate Donahue Berryman. Reprinted by permission of Farrar, Straus and Giroux, LLC. "Dream Song 241" and "Dream Song 384" by John Berryman, from *77 Dream Songs*. Reprinted with permission from Faber & Faber. ELIZABETH BISHOP: "For Grandfather" from *The Complete Poems 1927–1979* by Elizabeth Bishop. Copyright © 1979, 1983 by Alice Helen Methfessel. Reprinted by permission of Farrar, Straus and Giroux, LLC. SOPHIE CABOT BLACK: "To Her Father", "Turning Away" and "Brunnhilde, to Her Father" reprinted by kind permission of the poet. JOSEPH BRODSKY: "Odysseus to Telemachus" from *A Part of Speech* by Joseph Brodsky. Translation copyright © 1980 by Farrar, Straus and Giroux, LLC. Reprinted by permission of Farrar, Straus and Giroux, LLC. LUCILLE CLIFTON: Lucille Clifton, "cigarettes" from *The Book of Light*. Copyright © 1993 by Lucille Clifton. Reprinted with the permission of Copper Canyon Press, www.coppercanyonpress.org. HENRI COLE: "Radiant Ivory" from *Middle Earth* by Henri Cole. Copyright © 2003 by Henri Cole. Reprinted by permission of Farrar, Straus and Giroux,

251

Wylie Agency. HOWARD MOSS: The Estate of Howard Moss: "Elegy For My Father" by Howard Moss. HARRYETTE MULLEN: "Father (Part 1)" by Harryette Mullen, from *Blues Baby: Early Poems*. Reprinted with kind permission of the author. RICHARD MURPHY: "Natural Son" by Richard Murphy. By kind permission of the author and The Gallery Press, Loughcrew, Oldcastle, County Meath, Ireland, from *Collected Poems* (2000). "Natural Son" by Richard Murphy. By kind permission of Wake Forest University Press, USA. HOWARD NEMEROV: "September, The First Day of School" from *Collected Poems* by Howard Nemerov. Reprinted with the kind permission of Mrs Margaret Nemerov. NAOMI SHIHAB NYE: "My Father and the Figtree" from *19 Varieties of Gazelle: Poems of the Middle East* by Naomi Shihab Nye. Text copyright © 2002 Naomi Shihab Nye. Used by permission of HarperCollins Publishers. SHARON OLDS: "Nullipara", "His Terror", "His Stillness", from *The Father* by Sharon Olds, copyright © 1992 by Sharon Olds. Used by permission of Alfred A. Knopf, a division of Random House, Inc. MARY OLIVER: "Poem For My Father's Ghost" from *Twelve Moons* by Mary Oliver. Copyright © 1972, 1973, 1974, 1976, 1977, 1978, 1979 by Mary Oliver. By permission of Little, Brown and Co. and the poet. GEORGE OPPEN: "Sara in Her Father's Arms" by George Oppen, from *Collected Poems*, copyright © 1962 by George Oppen. Reprinted by permission of New Directions Publishing Corp. MEGHAN O'ROURKE: "Ohio" and "Elegy for a Grandfather (1972)" reprinted by kind permission of the poet. ELISE PASCHEN: "Threshold" by Elise Paschen. Used with the kind permission of the poet. BORIS PASTERNAK: "Hamlet" (16 lines) from *Selected Poems: Boris Pasternak*, translated by Jon Stallworthy and Peter France (Allen Lane, 1983). Copyright © Peter France, 1983. PASCALE PETIT: "The Strait-jackets" from *The Zoo Father* by Pascale Petit (Seren, 2001). Reprinted with permission from Seren.